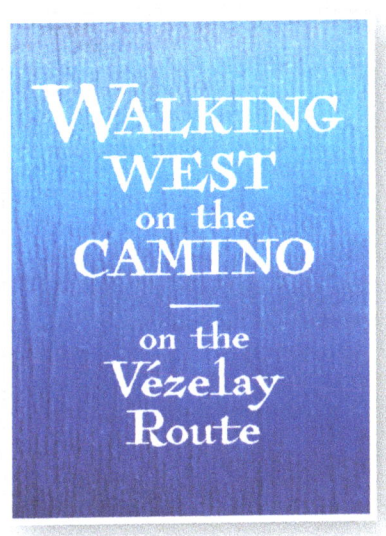

Johnna Studebaker

Walking West on the Camino—
on the Vézelay Route

Copyright © 2023

By Johnna Studebaker

www.johnnastudebaker.com
www.twopelerinespress.com

All rights reserved. No part of this book may be reproduced or transmitted in any form or by any means, electronic or mechanical, including photo-copying, recording, or by any information storage and retrieval system without the written permission of the publisher, except where permitted by law.

Text and Oil Paintings:
Johnna Studebaker

Book Design:
Kenesson Design

ISBN: 978-0-9992424-4-5

LCCN: 2023910430

Santa Fe, NM

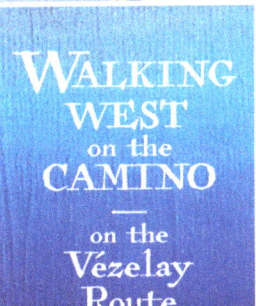

Acknowledgments

To my muse, the Holy Spirit, who walked with me and helped me all the way. To my friend, Barbara Taylor, who read my manuscript and gave me helpful advice and input and was always there to listen. To Grayson, my little hero, who taught me how to live courageously, and then, how to die. To Charlie Kenesson, my book designer extraordinaire; you are the best. To my sister, Marcia Pyner, who started out with me walking the Vézelay Route *ensemble* and then gracefully bowed to the Divine as I went on *seule*. To Mary Magdalene and to the Vézelay Route, who called me to them and whispered many things.

Contents

Acknowledgments iv

Introduction 1
    Under the Milky Way in Santa Fe, New Mexico 5

I.   **Summer 2019—Vézelay to Nevers** 7
    Painted from Jusepe de Ribera's *Magdalene Penitent* 11
    The Vézelay Basilica 17
    Basilica Glow 19
    Painted from *Our Lady of Vladimir* 25
    Left Toward Nevers 26
    Château de Domecy-sur-Cure 28
    Reaching Toward the Sun 31
    Cottage Dreams—in Bazoches 34
    The Blue Door—near Neuffontaines 35
    Poppies Along the Vézelay Route 38
    Chapelle Sainte Madeleine 54
    Painted from *Our Lady of Perpetual Help* 56
    Painted from Georges de la Tour's *The Penitent Magdalen* 57

II. **Spring 2020 to Summer 2022—The Valley of Tears** 59
    Autumn Stillness under the Crabapple Tree 63
    Chill of Winter at the Carmelite Monastery 64
    Au Printemps—Hope for a New Day 65
    Summer of 2022—The Camino Calls 66
    La Vie en Rose—Seeing life through rose-colored glasses 68

III. **Fall 2022—Nevers to Saint-Jean-Pied-de-Port** 69
    Along the Canal du Berry 76
    Just Past La Souterraine 80
    Marché de Rue—in Limoges 86
    Hôtel de la Lune—in Orthez 116
    Church of our Lady—Saint-Jean-Pied-de-Port 119

Epilogue 125

Introduction

Because strait is the gate, and narrow is the way, which leadeth unto life, and few there be that find it. Matthew 7:14

It was a cold, dark mid-winter's eve in 2018, in Santa Fe, New Mexico. I had awakened to a restless urge to walk The Way of St. James once more. In dismay, I pulled the covers up over my ears and tried to lull myself back into slumber, but to no avail. I had been dreaming again, of course, of the Camino. I could hear its plaintive cry, but this time calling me to the Vézelay Route. And, that restless wanderer in me had now prodded me into a waking state of clarity and pressing urgency. *She awaits you—when will you join her*, it whispered. How could this be, I wondered. My sister Marcia and I were barely home from our travels on the Camino. We had walked the Le Puy Route through southern France across the Pyrenees and then the *Camino Francés* (French Road) to Santiago on the northwest coast of Spain. Trekking in fog and mud into Santiago de Compostela that last day, we had both decided, most emphatically, that this was going to be our last adventure on the Camino. Enough is enough. *Fini!* We had walked roughly a thousand miles over a period of six years. Isn't that enough for any sane human to do in one lifetime? Well, apparently not. A rhetorical question, I guess, and silly me anyway, to think that the Camino might leave me in peace, merely to ponder its mysteries.

I parted the curtains slightly behind my head and peered out the window up to the parade of twinkling stars in the night sky.

The moon was full and bright, and it was as if the Milky Way had burst forth just for me. I thought about who might be walking the Camino right now under those stars—perhaps even with St. James, unawares.

The road to Santiago de Compostela is an ancient pilgrimage route which is third in importance and popularity only behind the routes to Jerusalem and to Rome. The relics of Saint James are said to be buried at Santiago. James the Great, the brother of John, was believed to be the first martyred apostle, beheaded by Herod Agrippa. The Apostle James had returned to Jerusalem after spending time evangelizing on the Iberian Peninsula. Legend has it that after he was beheaded, his body was secreted away from the Holy City by his disciples in a stone boat. The boat eventually landed in Padrón on the Galician coast of northwestern Spain. The story goes that about 812 A.D., a hermit named Pelayo, led by a bright star and celestial vision, found what was thought to be St. James' tomb in a Roman cemetery in Galicia. The tomb was discovered under a mantle of stars along the path of the Milky Way. And so sprang up the great cathedral at Santiago de Compostela "campus stellae" meaning in Latin "field of the star".

I smiled to myself for clearly the Camino was not finished with me yet. And as I finally drifted back into dreamy sleep, I too was walking the Camino—but now on the Vézelay Route. *Pas fini!*

Just what would possess anyone to walk the Camino—this path under the stars? In the Middle Ages, saints and sinners made the trek from across Europe—for penance, for a miraculous cure, for wisdom and spiritual awakening, for adventure. Prisoners were sentenced to the Camino. Paupers and princes came. The Roman Catholic Church and the monks from the Benedictine Abbey in Cluny in France were quick to sanction the site of Saint James, and they extracted favors and dispensations for the remittance of sins for the completion of the Way of St. James. They also most likely lined their own coffers. It was a motley crew that stepped forth to walk the Camino. And now, with the revival of this great pilgrimage in modern times, I too can be counted as one who has followed in their footsteps along the same medieval path, as well as hundreds of thousands more. I have come because I have been called to walk it over and over for reasons I do not know—inexplicable reasons. It, simply put, feels like home. I have dragged my twin sister Marcia along with me to the point that she too calls the Camino home.

Early in the twelfth century, as the pilgrimage route to Santiago de Compostela began to flourish, the *Codex Calixtinus*, a Latin manuscript named for Pope Calixtus II, came into circulation thus increasing its popularity even more. And probably that was its design. *The Codex* (*Liber Sancti Jacobi* or the *Book of Saint James*) extolled the importance of the shrine at Santiago and its relics. More specifically for our purposes, the final chapter, called *The Pilgrim's Guide*, gave practical information to help those pilgrims who ventured forth avoid the pitfalls of the journey. Most likely written by one named Aymeric Picaud, a Benedictine cleric from Poitou in France, the *Guide* lists holy sites to visit, places to find food and shelter, as well as other helpful tips for safe passage along the route. For example, one section warns the unsuspecting pilgrim to steer clear of a certain riverbank where unsavory locals were purportedly lying-in wait for a hapless pilgrim's horse to drink the river's contaminated water, then only to fall prey to those rogues and robbers on its banks. And then there are those unscrupulous boatmen who extracted large sums to ferry pilgrims across two rivers near the village of Saint-Jean de Sorde. Their boats were made out of single tree trunks, and heaven help the poor pilgrim who sat balancing precariously on that makeshift raft for fear he might fall in, his horse swimming behind it.

The Knights Templars, an order of warrior monks, who were fresh from their exploits in Jerusalem, began to guard the route. Pilgrim hospitals and hostels sprang up to house weary travelers and to minister to the sick and injured and dying. The pilgrimage to Santiago de Compostela also aided the cause of the re-conquest of Spain from the Moors during the Spanish Crusades. Saint James became the "Moor slayer", *Santiago Matamoros* in Spanish, and was depicted riding his great steed with his sword hoisted high in battle. He was also portrayed as the pilgrim, *Santiago Peregrino* in Spanish and *Saint-Jacques Pèlerin* in French, treading the path with his scallop shell and his staff, as he called the faithful to repentance and prayer. The popularity and importance of the pilgrimage route had reached a fever pitch. And, since its revival and designation as a UNESCO World Heritage Site in 1987, the Camino remains ever popular today.

Perhaps those who walked the Way of St. James in even earlier times found their way west by plotting the stars. By day, they would have followed the migratory pattern of flocks of geese traveling east to west. Of interest is what came next. Inspired by the pilgrimage to Santiago, an immensely popular board game called the Game of the Goose, *El Juego de la Oca* in Spanish and *Le Jeu de L'oie* in French, came onto the scene across Europe. Its creation was attributed to the Knights Templars who had designed the game as an esoteric path toward illumination. The object of the game was to reach square number sixty-three along a spiral path fraught with obstacles and danger. The number sixty-three reduces to the number nine, meaning completion, in numerology. In a more recent version, the pilgrim, his staff in hand, sets out, but he soon encounters a bull who tosses him into the air. As he continues, a goose accompanying him, he crosses a long bridge and then climbs a steep path upwards. He reaches a square where the sun shines brightly above him, but he then must carry on to a labyrinth, a well, castles, crosses, and cathedrals. For those modern-day pilgrims who have walked the path, doesn't that just sound familiar. Several squares depict the roll of the dice symbolizing a game of chance and synchronicity along the Camino and the path of life, in general. In fact, perfect timing is at play here as in all things. *Ca tomb bien.* If he is fortunate and has sought wisdom as his guide, the brave pilgrim has bypassed the death square where a skeleton pilgrim is depicted leaning on his staff presumably waiting for him with anticipation and glee. Courage, *Monsieur!* Or should I say *Madame.* Press on. At the game's center stands the great Cathedral at Santiago, the moon

Walking West on the Camino—on the Vézelay Route

Under the Milky Way in Santa Fe, New Mexico

and sun and stars shining above it in an azure sky. At its base sit two scallop shells, the iconic symbols of the Way of St. James. No wonder its widespread popularity. It is a hero's journey of initiation and an encrypted code to the mysteries of the Camino. One not lost on me.

The Pilgrim's Guide describes four routes to reach St. James through France. They converge near Ostabat in the Basque country where they join the *Camino Francés* to Santiago. They are the Paris Route, the Le Puy Route, the Arles Route, and the Vézelay Route. The *Voie de Vézelay, Via Lemovicensis* in Latin, begins southeast of Paris in Burgundy at Vézelay and goes through central France to eventually reach Saint-Jean-Pied-de-Port. St. Jean sits at the base of the routes crossing the Pyrenees into Spain. In December 1998, the Vézelay Route, which is approximately 558 miles long, was registered as a UNESCO World Heritage Site. The relics of Mary Magdalene are said to be housed at the *Basilique-Sainte-Marie-Magdeleine* in Vézelay. But I am getting ahead of myself down that treacherous road of intrigue and legend. So let us begin. Come walk with us again. Or should I say, *leap* fearlessly from that precipice like the Fool card from the Tarot, her sack flung over her back. Ride the wind along with us beneath the dark starry sky. For we know now that the net will surely appear.

Buen Camino! Bon Chemin!

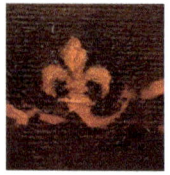

I.
Summer 2019
Vézelay to Nevers

65.1 MILES—7 DAYS

Vézelay, Domecy-sur-Cure, Le Chemin (Municipal Anthien), Guipy, Saint-Révérien, Breuil (Municipal Prémery), Guérigny, Nevers

Noli me tangere—Touch me not, for I have not yet ascended.
John 20:17

The chaos of the Dark Ages had given way to the establishment of a Christian Empire under Charlemagne, King of the Franks, in the early Middle Ages. And, as the Middle Ages progressed, its system of feudalism brought more predictability and order to the land so that pilgrims, or anyone else for that matter, could venture forth with some amount of assurance of safe passage. The Age of Chivalry had arrived in medieval Europe, along with knights and lords and serfs.

Within this context, the Basilica at Vézelay claims a fascinating and turbulent history. The new Abbey, founded by Count Girart of Roussillon around 860, was originally constructed to accommodate an order of nuns. The Abbey and monastery, a Marian shrine, stood just south of what is currently Vézelay in the tiny village of Saint-Père. The Abbey, later sacked by Norman invaders, was moved to the hill nearby where it might find added protection. We are told that Benedictine monks took up residency thereafter and thus replaced the nuns. And, as the pilgrimage to Santiago began to flourish, so also did the "cult of Mary Magdalene". The Abbey at Vézelay became a pilgrimage site, not just as a starting point for the Camino, but also as a shrine to venerate Mary Magdalene and her relics there.

Conflicting accounts developed about just how the relics of Mary Magdalene curiously ended up at Vézelay. Although there is some evidence that Mary Magdalene, along with St. John and Mary, the mother of Jesus, fled to Ephesus after Jesus was crucified and that she was buried there, another legend began to permeate the very fabric and culture of southern France that is still popular to this day. Early manuscripts claimed that Mary Magdalene fled Jerusalem along with her brother Lazarus, her sister Martha, Saint Maximin, and others to eventually reach the Mediterranean coast of Provence in southern France. She initially spent time near Aix en Provence preaching and performing miracles, but she later withdrew as a hermit and spent the last thirty years of her life in a cave near Baume. Lazarus reportedly traveled on to Marseille where he became the first bishop and was later martyred there for his Christian faith.

So the story goes, in the mid-eighth century, an early Abbot sent a monk named Badilus (or Baudillon) to collect Mary Magdalene's remains (relics) which were brought to the Abbey at Vézelay for safe keeping, just as the Saracens began to pillage southern France. By the early eleventh century, the new Abbot Geoffrey was installed at Vézelay by the powerful Cluny Monastery to bring much-needed reforms to the then lax religious house. The strict Rule of St. Benedict concerning celibacy and monastic order was reestablished. The pilgrimage to Santiago de Compostela and the Magdalene shrine were also both heavily promoted. In 1058, Pope Stephen IX confirmed the relics of the Magdalene to be authentic thus furthering the cause. Pilgrims began to flock to Vézelay. But, by the early thirteen century, Count Charles of Anjou excavated the tombs at the Church of Saint–Maximin in Provence and declared that Badilus had taken the wrong corpse and that the Magdalene did indeed lie in repose in Provence. Both sites were, most likely, vying for recognition and for the alms that might ensue. The relics at Vézelay, whose legitimacy were now in question, fell out of favor.

But just who was Mary Magdalene, she who is perhaps the most enigmatic female figure in the New Testament? Was she the repentant prostitute as has been her legacy across time? Interesting enough, Mary Magdalene is mentioned twelve times in the canonical gospels of Matthew, Mark, Luke, and John, more than any other woman, but never is she called a prostitute. She was described in Luke as one of certain women who had been healed of evil spirits and infirmities by Jesus: "Mary called Magdalene, out of whom went seven devils." She might have also been a woman of means because Luke goes on to describe these women who" ministered unto him their substance" and thus probably traveled with Jesus and the disciples and helped to support them—Mary Magdalene, Joanna, and Susanna. Luke: 8:1-3

The Synoptic Gospels of Matthew, Mark, and Luke give varying accounts of a woman who entered the home of the Pharisee, Simon the leper, in Bethany with an alabaster box and tearfully anointed Jesus' head with spikenard, a precious perfume, and wiped his feet with her hair. When the disciples complained in indignation that the expensive ointment could have been sold instead to help the poor, Jesus answered that she did it for his anticipated burial and then went on with a cryptic prophecy, "Where so ever this gospel shall be preached in the whole world, there shall also this, that this woman has done, be told for a memorial of *her*." Matthew 26:13; Mark 14:9 Later, in Luke, this unnamed woman is now described as a sinner.

Jesus said, "Her sins which are many, are forgiven; for she loved much." Luke 7:47 It is only the separate and distinct Gospel of John that identifies this woman as Mary, who at the home of Lazarus, in Bethany, anointed Jesus with costly ointment. John 12:3

Pope Gregory I, in a sermon preached in 594, claimed that the sinful woman mentioned in Luke was, indeed, Mary Magdalene. In the sermon, he suggested that she used the perfumed unguent on her flesh in forbidden ways, thus solidifying her legacy as a prostitute. But then, how else might a woman sin in those days, especially from the perspective of a church hierarchy who insisted on celibacy among its priesthood. Mary Magdalene became the penitent prostitute. In 1969, the Catholic Church moved to rectify the situation in which she had been previously promoted as a prostitute with an apology from Pope Paul VI, but her reputation as such sadly persists to this day. Mary Magdalene was later declared a saint. Her feast day is July 22.

All four Gospels identify Mary Magdalene as a witness to Christ's crucifixion and resurrection. The Synoptic Gospels say she was present at his burial. Mary Magdalene is described as the first to see him at the empty tomb after the resurrection and to have famously mistaken him for a gardener. And, because Jesus told her to go and proclaim to the disciples what she had seen, she is known as the "apostle to the apostles". John 20:15-17

This might be all we know of Mary Magdalene, but for the discovery in 1945 of ancient Coptic scrolls rolled in an urn and found in a cave in the desert in Egypt. Called the Nag Hammadi Library, these parchment scrolls are believed to be written in the second or third century and might even predate the Four Gospels. Called apocryphal or gnostic gospels (*gnosis* in Greek meaning knowledge), they were omitted by the Council of Nicea in 325 from the collection of texts that later became The New Testament. They were also banned as heretical and later stamped out by the Inquisition. Additionally, the Dead Sea Scrolls, found in caves at Qumran about the same time brought even

Walking West on the Camino—on the Vézelay Route

Painted from Jusepe de Ribera's *Magdalene Penitent*

more information to light about early Christian communities (including the Jewish ascetic sect of the Essenes) and their beliefs that were outside the now well-established orthodoxy of the Roman Catholic Church. The Cathars, a medieval Christian sect called "Pure Ones", endeavored to follow Jesus's simple teachings. Bernard of Clairvaux was sent to examine the heretics and found no fault with them. Nevertheless, in 1244, at the foot of Montsegur in southern France, 205 men, women, and children were burned at the Inquisition stakes, thus culminating what was called the Albigensian Crusade.

The Gospel of Philip, one of the Nag Hammadi texts, describes Mary Magdalene as Jesus' *koinônos* (Greek for partner or companion). Badly fragmented, the text most quoted reads that "(Christ) loved Mary Magdalene more than all the disciples and used to kiss her on (the mouth)." Highly speculative and controversial, various Biblical scholars have attempted to explain this passage away; others argue for its legitimacy based on its plain language. It has fueled much debate as we shall see as we proceed.

But there is more. The Gospel of Mary Magdalene, dated from the early fifth century and written in Coptic, showed up in an antiquities market in Cairo in 1896. It was purchased by a German scholar, but then languished without translation or publication in English until it was finally brought forward in 1975. Two earlier fragments found of the same text, written in Greek, date to the second century. Badly damaged, the Gospel of Mary Magdalene is comprised of seventeen pages, only half of which are intact. In it, Jesus warns the disciples to beware and not be led astray by those who might attempt to lay down rules or laws other than what he had given them. He emphasized that the Kingdom was within, and those that seek it would find it— self-empowering, to say the least, which most likely brought hope to so many early Christians.

In another segment, Mary Magdalene tries to comfort the disciples just after Jesus has ascended. Peter asks her to tell them what she could remember that Jesus might have imparted only to her, since he greatly loved her above all other women. Mary Magdalene went on to tell them what Jesus had taught her in mystic visions. But Andrew called the teachings she gave strange, and then Peter angrily complained that these teachings of Jesus had, after all, come from a *woman*. Levi then stood up and answered in support of Mary Magdalene who wept in sorrow at their treatment of her. Noting that Peter had always been hot tempered, Levi goes on, "If the Savior made her worthy, who are you, indeed, to reject her? Surely the Savior knows her very well, that is why he loves her more than us."

Scholars have been debating this newly discovered material and its possible implications on the development of early Christianity for decades. And yes, dear readers, I have diverted us from the Camino on a wild goose chase in search of Mary Magdalene before we have even begun. But I would have been remiss if I had not tried to untangle the web of misinformation and confusion that is the Magdalene. Was she, as well as other women who followed and even traveled with Jesus, intentionally left out of early Christian history and doctrine? We will never know, of course, who this Biblical figure really was for she is lost in time and mystery. I have wanted to do her justice, however, and round out her story in ways the four Gospels never did. You weren't hijacked for very long. Now let's get back on the Camino again, this time to start our journey to the *très magnifique* Vézelay Basilica.

It is late afternoon one steamy, hot summer's day in early June of 2019. I have been waiting for several hours now to meet up with my sister Marcia in the airport in Atlanta. Not always the patient sort, I have begun to pace the halls of the international terminal. And then there she is, like a mirage, smiling and waving and headed my way down the long corridor. When Marcia finally arrives, we are ecstatic to see each other. What we thought would never be again, to walk the Camino, is manifesting right before our very eyes into our shared experience once more. Yes, blame me for it. Our backpacks are lighter this trip. We know better than to bring hair dryers and camping pots, although I find myself even now gazing longingly at that glossy mini travel hair dryer displayed in the store-front window straight in front of me, in one of the many shops in the airport lounge area. Fortunately, temptation has no pull. Each of our packs weigh roughly ten pounds altogether, and when we add water, snacks, cat food, and picnic lunches, maybe twelve or thirteen pounds. We are both officio expert pilgrim packers. Plastic baggies filled with necessities and tightly rolled up clothing, for our excursions off the Camino, have been carefully stuffed into our bags. I am so excited.

By the time we reach Charles de Gaulle Airport in Paris, we are jet-lagged and exhausted, but we have no time to dilly dally. We disembark quickly and make a run for the local train RER B which will take us to the stop at Châtelet-Les Halles. We have purchased our fares from machines nearby with the help of a nice young station attendant who is intent on helping a crowd of befuddled travelers, not unlike ourselves, who are clamoring for his attention. So far so good. At our appointed stop, we jump off and head for the metro station and buy more tokens to get us through the turnstiles and onto Metro 14 and then, eventually, to the train station at Paris-Bercy. We have also become officio expert rail travelers, until we are not. I mean, until we get lost again or miss a connection because we have relaxed into overconfidence. My next life I want to be a bird.

At Gare de Bercy, we managed to get on the correct TER regional train heading for Sermizelles, the closest drop off to Vézelay. By now, pleased with ourselves, we settle into our seats for a nap and a power bar as we head for Sermizelles, two and a half hours away. But the Camino angels have already been working overtime, so it seems. Sometime during our train trip, we hear in broken English from a young French woman that our destination is Auxerre because the train does not stop at Sermizelles today as we had thought. *Oh la la!* At Auxerre, we

Walking West on the Camino—on the Vézelay Route 15

grab our backpacks and follow our nouvelle French guide onto a bus parked just outside the station, like lemmings rushing to the sea. Forty-five minutes later, after winding down hill and vale through the lovely French countryside and several small hamlets, we are dropped off at the Sermizelles train station. The station at Sermizelles is small and quaint and out in the middle of nowhere. It is also locked up. It is a five and a half mile walk from here to Vézelay. We sit down on the curb to assess our situation. The sweltering, unrelenting, late-afternoon sun has all but melted the pavement in places, it is so hot.

Just across from the station sits a lovely large country home painted in a French pale yellow. I walk over and knock at the door hoping we might get information about avoiding the long walk, via a taxi. A stately older gentleman appears in the door smiling, and seeing we speak a version of bad French, he motions for us to wait and disappears back into the house. Shortly thereafter, a young woman comes hurriedly around the corner, and, with a big smile and an out-stretched hand, she welcomes us in perfect English like we are old friends. She explains that she is an opera student with the master whom we had first met at the door. She is Marhiya Sora and can be found on YouTube singing soulful tunes and playing her guitar. Marhiya then kindly calls a taxi for us, and after a short wait, we are serendipitously whisked away down the road again toward our destination, in utter amazement. So goes our journey to Vézelay.

The taxi driver drops us off at a concrete barrier just at the entrance to the village of Vézelay. He explains, mostly by pointing and wild gyrations, that if we follow the cobbled street to the top of the hill, we will find the basilica. So now, our backpacks hoisted onto our shoulders, we walk the path upward past quaint shops and curios. Eventually, on the right, we reach the convent Saint Magdalena Center at 26, Rue Saint-Pierre. We had emailed the nuns there before we left home about staying in their pilgrim accommodations tonight. No reservation was required, but they are not checking pèlerins in yet, so we gladly deposit our packs in the small kitchen set up for pilgrims and continue our climb uphill. Fortunately, the basilica is open, but the whole front facade is covered in scaffolding—not enough to dull the beauty of this holy shrine. It fairly seeps with history and legend.

The eleventh–century Romanesque *Basilique-Sainte-Marie-Magdeleine* stands high in its resplendent glory against the backdrop of the bright blue sky as though it were reaching for those few little clouds floating just above it. It didn't always look like it does now. At one point, a fire destroyed much of the old abbey. A thousand pilgrims were killed. Rebuilt, the basilica was almost destroyed again in the sixteenth century by the French Huguenots in the Wars of Religion between the Protestants and Catholics. The French Revolution also took its toll. The famous French architect Viollet-le-Duc is credited with restoring the basilica to its present form in the mid-nineteenth century. The Basilica of the Magdalene is known for its distinctive striped arches in the nave or main interior, its Gothic choir, and most specifically, the Tympanum of the Pentecost at the entrance to the nave, called the narthex.

The Tympanum, carved in stone, depicts Christ in Majesty with the apostles. His arms outstretched, Jesus proclaims the mission to preach the Good News concerning the Kingdom. Early pilgrims, most likely, heard his call for renewal and transformation as they began their pilgrimage to Santiago. Spiral designs and the signs of the zodiac encircle the Tympanum symbolizing the constellations and the dance of the seasons. Notably, Taurus the bull stands there among the others, persevering in the face of challenges. The phoenix, associated with Greek mythology, is at the top of the Tympanum; the phoenix dives into the depths of darkness in the underworld, only to return transformed. So begins initiation. The glow of the basilica inside is haunting and overwhelmingly beautiful. The lights from the high pillars along each side of the nave have transformed the interior into dancing shadows throughout. We sink into a pew in silent awe trying to take it all in. As my eyes adjust to the dim light, I am drawn to

Walking West on the Camino—on the Vézelay Route 17

The Vézelay Basilica

the right side of the nave to a life-size statue of Mary Magdalene who is surrounded by glimmering candlelight. She stands stately and serene, holding the alabaster jar. I wonder if she might have known that her story of devotion and love for the Master would be told and retold ever after. In time, we make our way carefully down a set of stairs to the crypt where the purported relics of the Magdalene are displayed.

Having returned to the naïve, I am bombarded by images and sounds lingering from the old Abbey's rich history. According to *l'histoire ancienne de France*, the Gauls or early Celts had developed grid lines, called ley lines, which were aligned with the rising sun of the summer and winter solstices, to lay out their sacred structures. At the Vezelay Basilica, on the summer solstice, dancing orbs appear down the middle of the aisle in the nave. At the winter solstice, the sun casts its attention on the basilica's ancient capitals which crown the columns running down both sides of the sanctuary. By the mid-twelfth century, at the invitation of King Louis VII, Saint Bernard of Clairvaux preached his powerful Easter sermon at Vézelay, which launched the Second Crusade to the Holy Land. Fifty years later, the Third Crusade was launched here by the French King Philippe Auguste and Richard the Lionheart of England against the famous

Walking West on the Camino—on the Vézelay Route

Basilica Glow

muslin leader Saladin. The excitement and clamor of the events are palpable.

In the early thirteenth century, Saint Francis of Assisi founded the first Franciscan convent on the "eternal hill" at Vezelay. Later, King Louis XIV, the Sun King, most likely visited the Abbey there since his great military engineer, Vauban, kept a chateau nearby in the mountainous area of the Morvan.

As I am drawn back into the present moment, we realize we must retrace our steps quickly back down the hill to arrange our beds for the night at the convent. The afternoon sun is retreating behind the mountain, and *first come, first served* is hardly a reassuring thought. Fellow pilgrims are already congregating at the door of the convent eager to secure a bed for the night— we join their ranks. As pilgrims, we pay a donation of twelve euros each (about fifteen dollars) for a bed, a shower, and *petit déjeuner*. Fortunately, mission accomplished, we reclaim our backpacks and climb steep, circular, stone steps up a tower to our dormitory room. A pelerine from Sweden has already arrived and laid claim to a single bed by the window. In good English, she explains that her husband is next door in the facility set up for the men. Marcia and I choose two single beds across from hers. Along the other wall stands a row of six bunk beds. I wonder if we might have a full house tonight given that the pilgrimage on the Vézelay Route is not so well known or well-traveled and, thus, refuges for pilgrims can be scarce. I have now spread out my things and am as happy as can be. On the wall next to my bed is a beautiful reproduction of a medieval Byzantine icon from Russia of the Madonna and Child, called Our Lady of Vladimir. Ironically, it is one I too have painted. And before I know it, I have surrendered to the peace of my little bed for a much-needed cat nap.

Rested, Marcia and I head out to explore the tiny village of Vézelay and to find a place to have an early supper. The town is bustling with tourists, and the cafés and outside bars are crowded and loud. People have staked out the limited spaces for happy

Walking West on the Camino—on the Vézelay Route 21

hour. Of course, dinner is served much later, but we have designs to be sound asleep by then at the convent. We have walked to the bottom of Rue Saint-Pierre and beyond. On our way back up, we duck into a pâtisserie and purchase two large *croissants*, just as the shopkeeper is closing his doors. Next, we find a small market nearby and gather up ham and cheese, as well as pilgrim supplies for our journey tomorrow morning. Back at the convent, we have our concocted supper sitting at the kitchen table amid lay volunteers, both men and women, who are helping the nuns. There is a lively discussion about what to expect as we step out on the Camino—as if they might know. We silly humans just think we make the plans, but they can all go askew at the very next turn in the road, usually for the better—well, eventually.

Every bed is taken. Backpacks and hiking boots are lined up marking each spot. Our compatriots are out eating or shopping, because we have the large dormitory room all to ourselves right now. It is a welcome relief from a busy day. Tomorrow morning, after a quick breakfast, we will be up at the basilica early for the pilgrim mass. Soon, Marcia and I have both drifted off into a deep sleep.

⚜

I must have slept through the hubbub last night when our roommates returned to our dormitory room. I heard not a peep. This morning, the early sun is already shining through the two small windows nudging us all out of our beds. Soon enough, we have gathered around the kitchen table for strong French coffee, toasted baguettes, and homemade jam. We have packed up all our things, and our backpacks are outside in the courtyard awaiting our return from mass. No one worries about theft here; it is the pilgrim way. We are not prepared for the majesty and solemnity of the mass—it is so beautiful. Both nuns and monks are participating *ensemble* at the front of the nave, praying the liturgy and saying other special prayers. Their voices then ring out in chant and song in a blended harmony fit for the angelic realms. What we learn later is that the *Fraternités Monastiques de*

Jeruselem, an order of monks both men and women, have been in residence here at the basilica since about 1993, a fitting tribute to those early followers of Jesus, the One who welcomed all. Those pilgrims who are setting out this morning are called to the front, in French, and are being blessed and presented with tiny silver pendants of Mary Magdalene. The parishioners seated behind us, with their big smiles, have motioned us to join the others at the front altar. Tears welling in my eyes, I wonder how many thousands before us have been honored in this way as they, too, prepared to leave this great old abbey church at Vézelay, a place dedicated to the remembrance of the Magdalene, on the Way of Saint James.

Back again at the Saint Magdalena Center, we prepare to leave. Others are packing up or have already left. As we walk out of the courtyard, I turn back for one last glimpse of the convent and notice for the first time a lovely pink rose vine that has climbed the stone tower by the dormitory entrance. In fact, roses, the mystical icon of the divine feminine, are everywhere—along windowsills and bursting out of flowerpots by the door. Why had I not noticed them until now? As we walk down the narrow cobblestone street heading out of this lovely medieval village that is Vézelay, I find myself deep in thought. I am reminded of another legend surrounding Mary Magdalene that has flourished in the South of France for almost two thousand years. It is said that among those that came ashore on the marshy Camargue coast in the small rudderless boat with Mary Magdalene was a young dark-skinned child name Sarah, called "the Egyptian". To this day, in Saintes-Maries-de-la-Mer, relics of the three Marys and a statue of a black madonna are venerated. And the Grail Heresy, the legend of a holy bloodline (in Old French *sangraal* from the union between Mary Magdalene and Jesus, has fueled religious and cultural wars, as well as conspiracy theories, to this day. It is claimed that the Merovingian kings descended directly from this royal bloodline. And, in the Languedoc and in Provence, the troubadours and poets poured out their devotion to their Lady, to the feminine, and to courtly love in their fables of The Holy Grail. King Louis XI of France, believing himself to be of this holy lineage and entranced with the Magdalene legend, walked the Camino off and on for over thirty years.

Interestingly enough, on the feast day of Mary Magdalene, the Catholic Church extols the story of the Sister Bride searching for her Beloved from whom she has become separated, from The Song of Solomon, as did Saint Bernard in his own sermons. "I am black, but comely, O ye daughter of Jerusalem…" The Song of Solomon 1:5 Do those black madonnas, prevalent in churches across western Europe, symbolize certain hidden or esoteric truth about the sacred feminine? Oh dear, I have shaken the apple tree again when I promised to move on. And so we shall. Marcia and I have left the village and have followed the yellow and blue markers for the Vézelay Route to a crossroads. If we go right, we take the route through Bourges, and, if we go left, we are on the southern variant route through Nevers. The paths converge one hundred and eighty miles later in the village of Gargilesse. We turn left, for reasons you will see as we carry on.

The magnificent twelfth-century Gothic Bourges Cathedral, dedicated to Saint Stephen, is a UNESCO World Heritage Site like the Vézelay Basilica. Researching the cathedral before we started our journey, I was most interested in seeing its resplendent, brightly colored stain glass windows. But alas, we have chosen the Nevers route instead. We had read that the route through Nevers, with its more varied and hilly terrain, would eventually lead us to the Convent of the Sisters of Charity in Nevers where we would come face to face with the incorrupt body of Saint Bernadette. Now how could we resist such a spectacle as that? I mean no disrespect to St. Bernadette of Lourdes who spent the last years of her young life at the convent in Nevers. She has a fascinating story to tell which I hope to unravel once at Nevers.

Marcia and I are so happy to be walking the Camino again. There is a certain charm to the experience which is difficult to describe. Our path so far is taking us along a narrow, winding paved road through grassy fields of yellow, only disturbed by an occasional farmhouse or barn. The sky is bright blue with no clouds in sight. Besides following the yellow and blue markers posted on trees, we are using a walking guide published in English by the Dutch Association of Saint James which I had downloaded from the internet at home. We are guided onto a gravel road, a bank of red poppies on one side and an old split rail fence on the other. Diverted again, we are walking a dirt path amid a thicket of trees and high grass to reach eventually the small village of Saint-Père, its church spire heralding our arrival. It was a pleasant mile and a half stroll.

The Camino usually routes pilgrims by churches or cathedrals, and today is no exception. Soon enough we find ourselves at *L'Eglise de Saint-Père*, a beautiful old abbey church with its own rich history. We read inside that work began on the church in 1290 and was not completed until 1455. A much earlier abbey at St. Pere was transferred to the hill at Vézelay under the patronage of Count Girart de Roussillon and his wife Berthe. We stop to admire the pattern of diffused sunlight dancing down the aisle in the quiet cool of the nave. And then we go on, but not without casting a backward glance at those snarling gargoyles perched high on a stone column outside by the door.

Leaving the village, we walk down another narrow dirt path by farmland and woods and then through two hamlets until we finally reach a crossroads and become, well, hopelessly lost. Do we go back? Do we go on? Where are the waymarks? Where are we? And this is only our first day. There is no time for chatter and plenty of time for vigilance lest we head off in the wrong direction. Fortunately, we double back a bit and locate a little, overgrown footpath to our left which we had missed completely. No wonder. But first, we drop down on the small stone steps leading into the woods to share our packed lunch. I, unfortunately, in my haste to sit down, dropped our now unwrapped sandwiches on the steps. I hastily retrieve them like Pandora trying to get back what escaped from her box, thinking we can at least eat the side of our sandwiches that didn't hit the ground. Marcia isn't buying it,

Walking West on the Camino—on the Vézelay Route

Painted from *Our Lady of Vladimir*
(Byzantine icon, artist unknown)

Left Toward Nevers

and she missed out on our *déjeuner* all together. Me, I eat hers and mine both which, together, make one complete tasty sandwich, just like the good little enterprising pilgrim that I am.

This rising grassy footpath, described in our guidebook as "an ancient Roman road," brings us eventually back into civilization and to a paved road around a farm and the outer buildings of the lovely Château de Domecy-sur-Cure. By now, the heat of the afternoon is intense. We have reached the village of Domecy-sur-Cure, and although we have walked just under seven miles, we want to find shelter for the night here. The next village is over four miles away. I can't say that I am charmed with the Vézelay Route right about now, I mostly feel just plain hot and tired, no embellishments. We have found an address at the end of the village that reportedly provides beds and meals for pilgrims, but we were warned by our guidebook to call in advance which, of course, we have not done. We don't generally book in advance preferring to let the Camino arrange our beds. We also never know exactly how far we are going to walk each day, another reason making booking ahead difficult. No one looks to be home, and I am reluctant to knock at the door. Marcia knocks; there is no response. In retrospect, I realize we should have taken the advice of that nice young man who had come out of his house serendipitously just as we were passing by and had pointed to the home that took in pilgrims. I had distrusted his advice—the home looked so deserted. Had we been more persistent and waited, we might not now find ourselves retracing our steps through the village. We turn down a different road looking for signs for rooms or a *gîte d' étape* for pilgrims. At the end of this road, a woman comes out to tell us her small inn is closed. By now, Marcia has pointed out my beet red face and sweaty hair to me, so we reluctantly collapse in the grass to rest. As we head back from whence we came in circular fashion, a large dog suddenly runs up barking, followed by a woman hurrying behind him. We later decide she was sent directly to us from the heavenly realms. *"Bonjour, Madame. Comment allez-vous? Parlez-*

Château de Domecy-sur-Cure

vous anglais?" I manage to say. These are desperate times, and only my best French will do.

Between her broken English and our bad French, our nouvelle amie tells us she will ring her sister who has a *gîte* just down the street to see if she might provide us refuge. And before the booking angels can barely get back to heaven, we find ourselves settling in for the night at the sweetest spot ever. It is a cottage converted into a *gîte d' étape* for pilgrims. There were no signs for it, and we had walked by it at least twice in our traverse back and forth across the village. Marcia and I share a room with two single beds. We have the whole place to ourselves—no one else has booked here tonight. And since there is no restaurant or market in the village, before long, our dear amie delivers up pasta and marinara sauce and various other staples for us for tonight's supper and for *petit déjeuner* tomorrow morning, insisting we are not to pay them for the room or the meals. Then, her sister, with a gracious welcoming smile, pops her head in to check on us too. She explains they were in between rentals and had opened just for us. We plunk down our pilgrim donations on the kitchen counter, nonetheless, after they leave us, simply because gratitude must be played forward to enable its continued passage across the globe. I will remember the kindness of these sisters for the rest of my life.

⚜

Marcia and I are up early this morning. We have eaten toasted baguettes, homemade jam and butter, have had our café au lait, and have readied our backpacks to carry on. We have set our sights on Le Chemin (Municipal Anthien) and the *gîte l'Esprit-du-Chemin* which is owned and run by Dutch former pilgrims, Arno Cuppen and his wife Huberta. Our guidebook suggests we reserve the day before which, again, we have not done. It is almost nine miles away. We walk through the little village of Domecy-sur-Cure for the last time, and, at the bend, we are directed back onto that Roman road now described as a mountain bike trail. Three miles later, we emerge just behind the gates to the Bazoches

Castle. The *Château de Bazoches*, built in the twelfth century by feudal lords, stands on the edge of the Morvan, a vast area of protected wilderness and a national park. We would love to tour the castle, but it is closed until later in the day. The famous military engineer, Vauban, had once owned the castle and had turned it into a garrison where he worked on military projects there. He also wrote a famous treatise encouraging a single tax to help the commoners, thus incurring the great displeasure of King Louis the XIV. Fascinating history indeed.

As we descend along a wooded dirt road toward the village of Bazoches, we find ourselves walking through a most enchanting grove of tall trees. Their slender branches have formed a dense canopy of leaves high above us as they reach their long arms, clasped together, toward the sun. It feels like another time tunnel where, if you sit and wait for just a little while, time stands still. But we walk on, knowing the day is young and we must not tarry long.

Out of the woods again, we are walking through vast green fields and now down a small, paved road leading into the village. At the entrance to the village, we find a church we later discover to be *l' Église Saint-Hilaire de Bazoches* and the tomb of Vauban, located in a small side chapel. The gothic Church of Saint Hilare, completed in the twelfth century, ranks as one of the most beautiful old churches I have ever had the privilege to visit. Sunlight filters through the stained-glass windows depicting Jesus and Mary, making their robes glisten blue and crimson in the dark nave. Looking closer behind the front altar, we discover six life-size frescos, among them: Saint Joan of Arc, her blue skirts and armor ablaze; Saint Michael, his sword raised high above a demon; and Saint Roch, his humble pilgrim robe lifted slightly above his left knee showing the wound that never heals. And as if this was not enough, fleurs-de-lys and florets bedazzle the walls. They are painted hues of pink, green, lavender, orange, and blue. The Camino has, once again, served up such sublime and subtle beauty. It is no wonder I will walk it until the day I die.

Walking West on the Camino—on the Vézelay Route

Reaching Toward the Sun

Leaving Bazoches, we are afforded a lovely view of Vauban's majestic château sitting off in the distance. We continue down through more grassy fields and farmland along a winding dirt road passing, most notably, old stately stone crosses marking the Way of St. James. At one of these crosses, we stop to picnic on leftover baguettes and sardines. I might add that we have seen one fellow pilgrim on our walk so far, a lone elderly man who passed us by with barely an exchange. The Vézelay Route is the more contemplative path among the major Camino routes since it is the one less traveled. We can now attest to this. It also might be the most transformative. We are called to confront our fears about loneliness, food and shelter, even basic survival, and to exercise radical faith in the moment, not yesterday or tomorrow, but in the blessed now. Perhaps, the homeless and destitute on this planet, and there are many, might scoff at this notion of pilgrimage since they face these challenges and their own mortality every day. I look into a face of a panhandler walking the streets back home, knowing this might have been my face too.

We walk through the hamlet of Neuffontaines and then another hamlet to eventually reach our destination for the day, Le Chemin and the *gîte l'Esprit-du-Chemin*. Will our Dutch hosts be home, and is the place even open? I wonder, a bit apprehensively. Shortly, however, Arno Cuppen emerges from his back garden with a broad smile as if he were expecting us. Yes, the Camino whispers many things. Huberta, his wife, graciously shows us to a small room upstairs with two single little beds under the slanted eaves—it is perfect for us. A cheery window allows us to survey the property and gardens. We have plenty of time to shower, do some hand washing, and also to sit in the vast enclosed yard. This is a beautiful large farmhouse with blue shutters which, I imagine, come in handy against the cold winters when the *gîte* is closed. The surrounding old stone outbuildings are covered in trellises of red roses. And, to our surprise, a nun in full religious habit, probably in her eighties, has arrived on foot from the monastery at Vézelay for a late afternoon visit with

Arno and Huberta. She has walked fifteen miles in sandals, her face beaming with light and laughter at her journey's end. Arno arranges to drive her back by the end of the afternoon. If I were tempted to be just slightly envious of anyone, it might be of her; she is so uncompromisingly at peace.

By now, two friends of our hosts have arrived for dinner and to stay the night. We all sit down together to a summer supper extravaganza served on a long picnic table under the massive trees—French bread, an assortment of meats and cheeses, salad, pasta, and *sorbet de citron A votre sante!* It is a meal fit for a Queen and for two pelerines alike. In my little bed, I think, with gratitude, of all we have experienced this day and then nod off into blissful sleep.

This morning, the Camino, through Arno and Huberta, delivered some good advice: call ahead and book at Domaine d'Ainay in Guipy. Advice taken. Guipy is almost fifteen miles away, and the next refuge is five miles hence. After *le petit déjeuner* and hugs all around, we set out. We walk back up the asphalt road about two hundred feet and turn left at a cross down a small grassy footpath to regain the Route de Vézelay. The morning air is brisk, and it is a perfect time for a day's walk. Our path takes us through woods and forest for miles, finally to emerge at a white iron cross decorated in fleurs-de-lys. We are headed toward the village of Charpuis and then to Corbigny. We stop at a splendid old church in Corbigny, which has a lovely wooden statue of St. James, and then walk down the Grande Rue, cross a roundabout, and continue straight on via the Avenue Jules Renard toward the next village of Chitry. We are directed by our guidebook to turn right into a dead-end street and continue straight ahead, meaning we are about to enter the wilderness again. We are now on a gravel road (ancient Roman road) with a view of the seventeenth-century Castle of Chitry to our left. Once in the village of Chitry-les-Mines, we pass the Place Jules Renard and a monument honoring fallen soldiers. Here, we have our picnic lunch of bread and cheese and then walk on.

Cottage Dreams—in Bazoches

Walking West on the Camino—on the Vézelay Route

The Blue Door—near Neuffontaines

36 Summer 2019—Vézelay to Nevers

The heat of the day has finally caught up with us, but we are out of water, much less any shade, as we leave the village walking through the outskirts of town. We have literally sat down on the curb to rest, wondering how we can proceed in the heat without water. We both consciously and actively send out a prayer in unison for help. Neither of us wants to find ourselves again in a state of heat exhaustion as we did one summer while traveling in Mexico—it was scary. And I kid you not. Just at this time *en ce moment*, an iron gate at the house by which we sit opens, and a car eases out to leave. But, when this kind older man sees us sitting there, he stops and invites us into his home for water and respite. He is a veteran too, like our father who had been sent to France during World War II. He reminisces about those days in the war and shows us pictures of his deceased wife. We connect as though we were old friends. Is it a coincidence that he would pull out and stop everything to help us then? I think I know, but you decide.

We have almost six more miles to go to reach the Domaine d'Ainay where we have booked for the night with Madame Leyenhorst. At the village of Chaumot, we cross a bridge over a canal and enter dense woods again. Just to our left stands a particularly graceful old tree, his wide trunk clothed in moss. He sports his lapel pin, a Camino shell, on his mossy vest, as well as a small now familiar yellow and blue waymark pointing us straight on. We have had to be more vigilant on the Vézelay Route because, although there are markers, they are infrequent. We are always most happy to see them. He is *Monsieur L'Arbre*, another grand fellow and *nouveau ami* on the Camino. We wave *au revoir* as we pass him by, regrettably unable to sit for a chat, never to see him again.

Back on another paved road, we walk past what is described in our book as a "fortified farmhouse," Le Bouquin. Looking more like a castle, its towers and turrets gleam in the sunshine. We walk on into the village of Pazy and then later through Prélichy heading toward Guipy, our destination for this day. Is it

Walking West on the Camino—on the Vézelay Route

a mirage? We see an estate in the hazy heat way off in the distance and around the bend. About this time, a man in a car pulls over and confirms this is, indeed, our appointed destination, the Domaine d'Ainay, and asks us if he might drive us there. I guess we look rather bedraggled sitting in the dirt on the side of the road. But, of course, I refuse the invitation, probably from an angel, thinking we ought to walk and not cheat the Camino by accepting rides. Silly me. Walk and walk and walk we do, until we finally reach the compound into the early evening exhausted. *Mme. Leyenhorst* (Angela) runs down the long driveway to meet us waving excitedly and welcoming us in English, she who wondered if we would ever get there at all.

The Domaine d'Ainay is a large estate and country home in Burgundy. It has camping facilities and also operates as a bed and breakfast. We had no idea. There is also no pilgrim rate, but we soon see why. We are shown to our spacious private room, Chambre Billardon, which is beautifully decorated in antiques, paintings, and a grand fireplace. The exterior of the old home, painted a pretty yellow, has been renovated, but it has kept its original charm. The vintage, lattice-work shutters have been painted pale green. Its towers and silver-gray turrets glisten in the late day sun.

The Camino has done well to arrange our stay here, despite ourselves. Our dinner, roasted goose *avec pommes de terre et salade verte*, is served by

Poppies Along the Vézelay Route

Angela in the formal dining room. We learn later her husband is the chef. French guests for the night have joined us at the table, and we enjoy *vin rouge ensemble*, most likely produced and bottled at the estate. I ask Angela if she is familiar with the board game, Game of the Goose, which was popular in Europe for centuries, and she laughs and says she has the game in the attic. Oh, how I wish she could bring it down for us to see, but her evening is busy with their guests, and the moment slips away, as all moments do.

A delicious assortment of *pains au chocolat, croissants, et baguettes* piled high on plates on the table await us for *le petit-déjeuner*, along with steaming hot, dark roast French coffee, butter and blackberry jam. *C'est magnifique!* Turning our attention forward once again, we are already packed up and ready to leave. We have arranged a ride with two French sisters, who are also leaving this morning, to take us with them back up the road to the center of Guipy to reconnect with the Camino. I don't consider this cheating, but if it is, so be it. Actually, the Domaine d'Ainay is just off the Vezelay Route about a mile. Once dropped off, we follow directions from our guidebook and go left down Rue Saint-Jacques de Compostelle. Our goal this day is the small village of Saint-Révérien which is less than five miles away. We find ourselves walking down a dirt path through tall grass and vast areas of undulating farmland, eventually to reach the hamlet of Brèches and then Saint-Révérien.

We are staying at the *Refuge Pèlerin Municipal* located in the old postal and telegraph building to the right of the town hall on the square, *La Place de la Mairie*. A monument to those children killed in the First World War, surrounded with lovely red rose bushes, stands in the center of the square. Marcia punches a code listed in our book in order to get into the *gîte*, and sure enough, the door eases open to allow us entry. Word gets out quickly that we have arrived because, soon enough, a municipal caretaker arrives to check us in and receive our donations. For ten euros each, we have small single beds upstairs and full use of the house, including the kitchen. As with other gîtes along the Vézelay Route, we are the sole pilgrims. Having unpacked and showered, we prepare our early supper of pasta and marinara sauce and hang out in the grassy enclosed back yard until mass. As the sun sets and darkness comes, so does the rain.

The Romanesque *L'Église de Saint-Révérien*, located just off the town square, is a hop, skip, and jump for us, through puddles, to its doorstep. We are delighted to find a small group of parishioners already there. They easily welcome us to their prayer group and to sing the litany. The church is dedicated to Saint Reverianus who was executed by the Roman Emperor Aurelain in the third century along with about ten of his followers. Known as the "apostle of the Morvan," a statue of St. Reverianus holding his head stands just to the left of the nave in a side chamber. Interestingly, two rather grotesque murals surround him, one the skeleton of a man and the other of a woman in a nun's habit. This is a spacious, beautiful old church with other more colorful murals depicting Christ and also St. Joseph holding the baby Jesus. Unfortunately, some are fading into history. To the right of the door stands a lovely old statue of St. Joan of Arc dressed in silver armor. Also, we find two colorful stained-glass windows, one of Saint Bernadette kneeling before the grotto and the Blessed Mary, the other of Saint Margaret Mary Alacoque kneeling before the risen Christ. The community, more than tolerant of an occasional pilgrim passing through, welcomes us with an open heart as we sit with them in their circle of prayer and worship. This experience will remain with me, as well as Marcia, as another sweet memory on the Camino that will never fade.

Upon arising this morning, we enjoy our Starbucks instant coffee and an energy bar and then pack up to move on. We are heading for the village of Breuil and the *gîte* "*Un pas à la fois*" (one step at a time). We have managed to call ahead. We are only walking eight miles, but, somehow, searching for a place of refuge late into the afternoon seemed rather unappealing. Leaving the village, we are directed onto a small dirt road up another ancient Roman road marked by a colorful large rock painted "*Voie Romaine.*" It also marks our departure into the wilds of the deep woods. We eventually reach a clearing and a beautiful old cross.

We are headed toward Boulon on the *Route des Fontaines*. After walking through several hamlets, we reach Breuil, our destination. We are fairly unscathed and even spared by the rain. How might we know we have arrived? Well, pilgrim boots, painted bright red and yellow, are placed fancifully on top of a low stone wall in front of the cottage. *Bienvenue aux pèlerins*—welcome home! Our host, Mme. Jourdan (Chantal), checks our pilgrim credentials and passports and then shows us the kitchen and the upstairs bedrooms for pilgrims. Marcia and I stake out our two little single beds and unpack—didn't we just do this not long ago? Our room is cheery and bright, once again decorated in yellow and red. It is a warm afternoon, and we bask in the sunshine in the back yard before dinner. Chantal, in the meantime, has driven to Nevers and returned with her elderly mother who will be visiting for several days. Chantal has prepared a scrumptious meal of coconut chicken and couscous, along with *une salade verte, trois fromages*, and crème *glacée* for dessert. *Bon appétit!* At dinner, Chantal relates that she met her husband on the Camino, and, together, they built this gîte to accommodate fellow pilgrims

in an isolated area where few other refuges can be found. To say I am grateful for it might be an understatement. After dinner, I can barely drag myself back upstairs to bed. Marcia and I are planning our journey tomorrow based on our Dutch Association maps. Marcia wisely books ahead for a hotel in Guérigny at the suggestion of our host—it is almost fourteen miles away. Sleep comes easily for us both.

After café au lait and croissants with Chantal, we are out early once more. Dark clouds are gathering, and it smells like rain. We are headed toward the larger town of Prémery which is little more than two miles away. Our plastic rain capes and hiking gaiters have been strategically placed in the outer pockets of our backpacks for quick reach, if needed. Gaiters are a new addition to my backpack for good reason—plastic baggies may be my best friends, but mud is not.

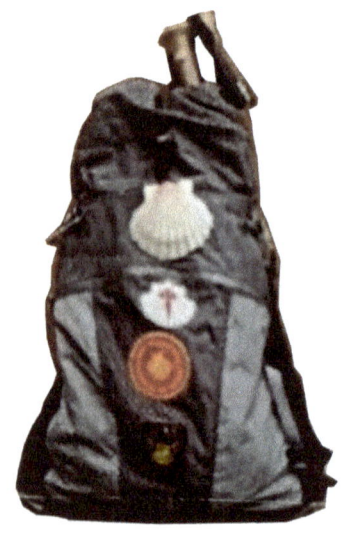

Walking West on the Camino—on the Vézelay Route

Here is my updated list of what I take on the Camino:

- backpack (in Europe, called a rucksack) the lightest one you can find—no frills; a hip belt is a must as are padded shoulder straps. My backpack weighs less than a pound.
- hiking sandals, for your sore toes when walking the Camino (and for evening strolls around the village or from table to bunk bed
- extra pair of underwear
- broad brimmed hiking hat (packable)
- plastic rain cape which covers body and backpack
- gloves
- one extra pair of hiking socks
- one extra blouse and pair of pants for after hiking (rolled up in a one-gallon baggie)
- one extra jacket stuffed in its own little bag (layer, layer, layer)
- silk sleeping bag shell, or any sleeping bag liner (yes, that's right—no sleeping bag, unless you go in winter)
- travel shampoo and conditioner, soap, shower cap, packets of laundry detergent
- small travel towel
- blister supplies, tweezers, nail clippers, travel blunt-end scissors, sunscreen, tissues
- walking guide
- smart phone (for the camera, emergencies, or to book ahead, if necessary)
- small flashlight
- hiking poles
- power bars and Emergen-C packets (packed in a one-pint baggie)
- mascara, lipstick, lip balm, blush (packed in a one-pint baggie)
- hiking gaiters *Pas de boue* (mud), *s'il vous plaît!*
- Wear good hiking boots and socks, hiking pants, a blouse or shirt, and a fleece or other lightweight jacket for early morning, depending on the weather and time of year. *Voilà!*

We are walking mostly down a narrow asphalt road to Prémery which is a bit of a relief from the wilds. Once there, we take the Grande Rue by the town hall as directed by our guidebook. We have also located a Carrefour or supermarket just off the Camino where we can happily replenish our supplies—mixed nuts, yogurt, bananas, apples, bottled water, cans of sardines, Babybel cheese, baguettes, and cat food. We are here over an hour; it is just such fun to browse a European market, in general, and to be in civilization, in particular. Donning our packs again (now much heavier, unfortunately), we carry on.

Leaving Prémery, we are instructed to continue straight ahead past factory buildings on the edge of town and then to continue on a gravel road up and then a dirt road up. The operative word is up. By now, it has started to drizzle, and we have hurriedly put on our rain capes and have wrapped our gaiters, secured with Velcro, around our lower pants legs. We eventually reach the D148, a paved winding road described in our book as "rising through the forest of Prémery" Be forewarned. I am usually not too worried on the Camino since we eventually reach hamlets and run into other pilgrims—not so here. It is quite desolate in the dense woods, and I am outside my comfort zone. It doesn't help that I notice a lone car drive by and then see it again parked nearby, here and there, in the distance, as we continue our trek up. I don't alert Marcia. Why should two of us be alarmed? We eventually reach the hamlets of Rigny and then Mauvron, both rather deserted, except for a stray cat. In the deluge of cold rain, la chatte has taken up with us inside the shelter of a school bus stop for *le déjeuner*. Lunch on God, so to speak. We are all three huddled in this dirty, graffiti-ridden hut, content as can be, dining on sardines and cheese and cat food for Mme. Kitty. *Pas de problème* Life has its sweet ironies, *n'est-ce pas?*

As the rain subsides, we walk on, to finally arrive many miles later at the Grande Rue, the main street in the village of Guérigny. The sun is out now, and we have located the Hotel Le Commerce, our oasis for the night. We have booked a small room with a double bed at the pilgrim rate. By evening, at their restaurant, we order from the pilgrim menu—fish and chips, *une salade verte, vin rouge,* hearty sliced bread, and *crème brûlée* for dessert. My only regret this moment is that *notre nouvelle amie,* Mme. Kitty, isn't here to join us. *C'est dommage!* Yes, it's too bad!

Tomorrow, we hope to reach Nevers, eight and a half miles away, our final destination this year for our time on the Vézelay Route. Both of us tonight spend some time doctoring our feet and toes for both old and developing blisters—oh, the joys of pilgrimage. I must be stark raving mad to walk the Camino year after year and to drag Marcia along with me. And these are my pleasant thoughts as I drift off to much needed sleep.

Up bright and early and refreshed, we have *le petit-déjeuner* in the hotel restaurant, pick up our sack lunches, and settle our bill. As we leave the village, we are directed onto a dirt road and then into more dense woods. We have crossed two different bridges over the Rive Nièvre and then have walked through several hamlets to reach, finally, the old provincial town of Nevers. Nevers sits on the bank of the Loire River at its convergence with the Nièvre. It was a lovely day for a walk and uneventful, thankfully, with no drama, well, until now. We are looking for the convent at *34 Rue Saint-Gildard* where we hope to spend the night before traveling back to Paris tomorrow morning. Both of us tired, Marcia wants to go one way and me the other to reach our destination. We finally locate the convent, after an hour or so, with some amount of grumbling and apologies (I won't say by whom). It's another sister act gone awry.

L'Espace Bernadette-Maison d'accueil Saint-Gildard and its *Hôtellerie* are open, much to our delight, and the nuns at the front desk are busy checking in guests, us being two of them. We situate our backpacks in our room which is located on the ground floor and then make our way to the chapel nearby where the body of Saint Bernadette lies in repose. In 1858, *Marie Bernarde Soubirous,* then just fourteen, met the Virgin Mary eighteen times, it is said, in dazzling visionary experiences, at a grotto in Lourdes. Throngs of people have visited the grotto ever since these Marian apparitions, and many have experienced healing there in its gurgling springs. Lourdes, located in southern France on its border with Spain in the Midi-Pyrénées not too far off the Camino, is a major pilgrim destination and shrine. Bernadette eventually joined the Sisters of Charity and lived out her short life at the convent at Nevers. Having contracted cholera as a child, she suffered from severe asthma most of her life. She died at age thirty-five from tuberculosis. She, like Jesus, emphasized the power of faith in the healing process. Many bright souls, it seems, die young; it is as if they fulfill their mission on earth and then go home.

We sit for a while in the quiet cool of the chapel and then view the relics of Saint Bernadette laid in a gold and crystal reliquary in a side chamber. Although her face and hands have been covered in a thin coat of wax, her body, exhumed three times since her death, remains largely incorrupt. I am struck by the peace and lightness of being in her countenance. She, dressed in the dignity of her nun's habit, is on display for all to see.

Leaving the chapel, we sit in the garden at the convent at the re-created grotto where a small statue depicting our Lady of Lourdes, dressed in the familiar blue and white, stands high in a crevice in the rocks beneath the kneeling Bernadette.

After a quick supper in town, we return to our little room quite content to go to bed early and to think of all we experienced this day. Bonne nuit.

Marcia and I have a wonderful *petit-déjeuner*, buffet style, at the small dining room at the convent and then race over to the train station nearby, lugging our packs. We are hoping to book passage early back to Paris. We are in luck and, soon enough, find ourselves whizzing through the countryside towards Paris Gare de Bercy on a SNCF regional train. Once at the Bercy station,

Walking West on the Camino—on the Vézelay Route 47

we locate the Metro line that runs closest to the Marriott on the west side of Paris and, eventually, reach the hotel, but not without some amount of angst in pulling it all off. I have mixed feelings about leaving the Camino—sadness, but also a sense of relief. We couldn't figure out how to arrange our limited time in France. Had we continued our trek, we weren't clear where or how we might get back to Paris in time for our flight home. I plan to continue on the Vézelay Route next summer and would prefer to have a longer block of time in which to walk it. Marcia has retired as a flight attendant from Net Jets, but I am still working full time as an attorney in Santa Fe. Getting time off for a couple of months to walk the Vezelay Route to Saint-Jean-Pied-de-Port, the gateway to the Pyrénées and Spain, almost five hundred miles, may have to wait until I, too, have retired. That time is closing in on me very nicely, actually. I have the will, but the way has yet to open, but so it shall.

Marcia and I split a hamburger and fries from the Marriott's bar menu and then turn in early. I think of those countless pilgrims in medieval times who could not leave the Camino and opt for clean sheets and a hot shower in a hotel. As I drift into sleep, I feel grateful for what I have and for what I don't have, like swollen ankles or broken bones or bug bites, much less attacks from bandits or beasts. And so it is, until next summer, when we will be back, hopefully, to continue down the path.

Marcia and I are heading to northwestern France this morning to the region of Brittany, to Rennes, on the train. Rennes is the departure point for day trips to a most unusual and fascinating sacred site that we have wanted to see for some time—the Abbey at Mont-Saint-Michel, a UNESCO World Heritage Site. But first, we must get there. We reach Rennes by late afternoon and book for two nights at the Novotel Gare Hotel which is close by the train station. Having settled in, we race back to a restaurant near the station and dine on an early supper of pizza, *salades verte, et verres de vin rouge*—we could do worse, much worse. It is drizzling rain now, heading quickly toward a deluge, so it becomes another race back to our hotel, but not before we book two tickets on an early bus for Mont-Saint-Michel for tomorrow morning. We have also dodged into a petit market for dog food, to feed that homeless dog we met on our way out to eat. Mission accomplished—supper on God. It is painful for us to cross the paths of stray dogs and cats without trying to help them, if just in passing. Back in our beds, sleep shows up quickly as we are lulled by the patter of the rain.

This morning, dark clouds are gathering again as we make our way back to the station to catch the bus to the *Abbaye du Mont-Saint-Michel*. Mont-Saint-Michel is located about an hour's drive north of Rennes on the northern coast of France near the beaches at Normandy in the English Channel. The bus is full, and some are turned away. Now, as the sky unloads torrential rain, it barely dampens our excitement and anticipation. Although, I must say, as we wait out these sheets of cold rain in the shelter of the welcome center for visitors, our rain capes dripping wet, this point might be debatable. Eventually, we board a bus to take us across the sandy shoals and low-lying water to the abbey and the little village of Mont-Saint Michel that surrounds it. Ominously, the occasional crash of distant thunder and the rain have finally quashed our hopes to walk across the bay in the shallow water or on the long bridge and footpath.

Mont-Saint-Michel, called "the Gate to Heaven," has a long, fascinating history. What follows just scratches the surface. In 708, Bishop Aubert built a sanctuary on a rocky outcrop on what was then called Mont-Tombe to venerate the Archangel Michael. Saint Michael had, purportedly, come to the bishop in a dream or vision instructing him to build the monument. And so, the abbey became a pilgrimage destination in its own right.

It is likely that many English pilgrims, on their journey to Santiago de Compostela in the Middle Ages, also stopped here. By the fourteenth century, the Benedictines occupied the Romanesque abbey, by then, an important fortress and stronghold during the Hundred Years War with England. Later, a fire destroyed the abbey and village below. King Philippe Auguste of France, fresh from his pursuits in the Holy Land after the Third Crusade, had the old abbey reconstructed in the Gothic style with its characteristic buttresses used to support its massive weight. During the French Revolution, the abbey again fell into disarray and was used as a prison, housing thousands of prisoners at one point. By 1874, renovations began on it again carrying forward to today.

Marcia and I are dropped off by the bus just outside the ramparts high on the cliffs at Mont-Saint-Michel. Thankfully, the rain has stopped. Having purchased our entrance tickets, we walk the narrow, cobbled street below the abbey past the shops and climb sets of steep stone stairs, ever winding our way upward. Finally, we stand in awe in the silence of the nave at the abbey church high above the bustle of crowds of people below. A wooden statue of St. Michael greets us along one wall. He holds the scales of justice (a reckoning) in one hand and his sword in the other; the dragon writhes beneath his feet. A bas relief or flat stone sculpture of the Four Evangelists, dating from 1547, is mounted on a wall in a side chamber. We climb more stairs to the grand Guests' Hall where

the monks and clerics once received royalty and nobility. The old abbey and church were built high on the rocks fortified beneath by a series of pillared crypts and vaults; one is called the Saint Martin Crypt. Although interesting, the atmosphere is dark and foreboding, and even more so as we walk through a small passageway and enter the former monks' ossuary where bones were once stacked and preserved. To add to the ambience, a huge wooden wheel with pulleys occupies the center of the room. It was installed in 1820, we read, to hoist up provisions to those wretched souls whose misfortune it was to be imprisoned here. Prisoners trudged within the tread wheel to turn it to bring up supplies. To say the mood is heavy might be an understatement. As we climb down another dark narrow staircase, we come to the almonry on the first floor where the monks once received pilgrims of all classes, as well as the poor, to whom they must have given out alms. Another bas relief starkly depicts Bishop Aubert with Saint Michael standing over him piercing his skull with his finger. Apparently, it is a reference to the hard-headed, hapless bishop who initially resisted Saint Michael's direction to build the abbey until the saint came to him a third time in his dreams.

The "Merveille," the monks' living area and cloister, comprises a separate area at Mont-Saint-Michel. In the late eleventh century, Richard the First, Duke of Normandy, tried to return the monks, who were heavily influenced by favors from the local nobles, to piety. The duke decreed that the monks must accept the Rule of Benedict of prayer and work, a more monastic way of life, or leave. All but one monk left. Today, the Monastic Fraternities of Jerusalem, the same brilliant order of nuns and monks that is at the Vézelay Cathedral, occupies the monastery at Mont-Saint- Michel. Their influence and that of Mary Magdalene become more apparent as we reach the little *Chapelle Sainte Madeleine* which is nestled high in the rocks here. I am struck by the beauty of the diffused light that shines through a huge verdant-green stained-glass window at the front of the chapel. There is a repeating pattern in the stained glass of the alabaster jar as well as the scallop shell, so symbolic of the

Walking West on the Camino—on the Vézelay Route 51

Camino. It is as though we never left the Vézelay Route at all. We sit for a while in the cool dark of the chapel to ponder its subtle mysteries.

Leaving the monastery, we are afforded a beautiful view overlooking the bay and beyond to the coast of Britain. Looking up at the pinnacle of the abbey's spire, we find a dazzling, golden statue of Saint Michael the Archangel, his sword raised high. Walking down the Grand Rue, we dodge into a restaurant for, as it turns out, huge bowls of mussels I thought I had ordered salads for us based on what I saw being served in the dim light at the table next to ours—better to inquire next time.

The *Église Paroissiale Saint-Pierre*, called the Sanctuary of Saint-Michel, the Center of Pilgrimage in the fifteen and sixteenth centuries, is another beautiful and serene old chapel to our right as we are heading down the cobblestone main street to leave. An imposing life-size statue of Saint Joan of Arc, in full battle armor, stands just to the left of the outer doorway, as if she guards the entrance. Of course, Saint Michael is prominent in art here, but also, we find Saint Roch. Saint Roch, the patron saint invoked against the plague in medieval times, who was so beloved along the Camino especially in France even today, stands with his faithful dog at his side. Dressed in his iconic pilgrim cloak and hat, he lifts his robe showing the wound on his leg that

never heals. There is also magnificent art depicting Jesus and Saint Peter as well as the Blessed Mother and the Christ Child. It saddens me that I probably will never get back here again to sit in the silence and the presence of such beauty and light. These old chapels tell the tale of suffering and yet hope in the Divine for us mortals who can only look up and offer our prayers. Unfortunately, we cannot linger for very long. The afternoon is slipping by quickly, and we must carry on. Since the rain has stopped, we are able to walk across the bridge back to the welcome center where we catch a bus back to Rennes. As the sun sets, we have eaten an early supper and are tucked in our beds. Reflecting on this busy day brings peace as I drift off to sleep.

As usual, we are up early. We have a wonderful breakfast buffet at the hotel, including *croissants et pain* of all kinds, fruit, yogurt, boiled eggs and steaming hot *café au lait*. We linger for the love of the moment and then head out to explore Rennes. The city of Rennes is both modern and medieval. Avenue Jean Janvier takes us into a busy commercial district in the central city with its broad grassy promenade. We soon find ourselves walking through the old part of the city: cobblestone streets, restaurants, and shops. Unfortunately, everything is closed for now. At the *Place Toussaints*, All Saints Square, we happen upon another

Walking West on the Camino—on the Vézelay Route 53

beautiful church, *l'ancienne église Toussaints.* Inside, I am delighted to find a reproduction of the fifteenth-century Byzantine icon known as Our Lady of Perpetual Help. On the painting, Greek inscriptions mark the presence of the Archangel Michael and the Archangel Gabriel, both who carry the instruments of the crucifixion. My focus, however, is on the Blessed Virgin Mary, a Marian image that has brought me comfort for many years and which I have painted.

Finally, back at the hotel, we split an American-style hamburger and fries at the bar for an early supper and then turn in. We return tomorrow morning on the train to Paris for two nights. Pilgrims we are, most certainly. But we are also occasional happy patrons of the Charles de Gaulle Airport Hilton—a mix not lost on me.

Today, after much conversation and consternation as to how to spend our last day in France, we are heading by train to the *Château de Chantilly* which is located about thirty miles north of Paris. To back up, we have spent the night at the Airport Hilton and have now made our way across Paris on the Metro to the Paris Nord Station to board a train for a day trip to the beautiful castle of Chantilly. I feel like a child in a candy store. In fact, Chantilly is famous for not only the delicate Chantilly black lace that was once produced there, but also for its Chantilly whipped crème. Once in Chantilly, we jump on the local bus that eventually drops us off at the gates to the *Domaine de Chantilly* which comprises the chateau, its magnificent gardens, and an equestrian center. With a little luck, not to mention perfect timing, we are able to purchase our tickets at the gatehouse and run for the château just as the dark, cloudy sky releases its buckets of rain. *Ca tombe bien*

The Château de Chantilly has its own fascinating history. The estate itself dates back to 1484 and to the Montmorency family. In 1560, Anne de Montmorency, having already renovated the medieval structure there, also built the Petit Château. By 1643, Louis II de Bourbon-Condé, the Great Condé, one of King Louis

Chapelle Sainte Madeleine

XIV's greatest generals and his cousin, inherited the estate through his mother, Charlotte de Montmorency. Condé hired Le Notre, the famous gardener at Versailles, to create vast gardens and lakes on the estate, much to the delight of the guests there who must have enjoyed festivities and fireworks late into the night. He also hired François Vatel, the *maître d' hotel* and "royal caterer," to manage the delicacies in the kitchen. In 1671, the third day into festivities honoring the King, poor Vatel was so anguished at not receiving the fish he had ordered for the menu that night that he killed himself. The fish arrived later just in time for the festivities.

During the French Revolution, the Grand Château fell into the hands of the revolutionaries and was used as a prison until it was destroyed in 1799. By 1830, Henri d'Orléans, Duke of Aumale, the fifth son of King Louis-Phillipe and part of the Bourbon and Condé lineage, was bequeathed the estate. The Duke of Aumale rebuilt the Grand Château and added the *Musée Condé* to house his extensive and exquisite collection of paintings, furniture, and books. In his will, at the explicit instruction of the duke, the walls in his art gallery were painted red to showcase works of Botticelli, Raphael, Fra Angelico, and Delacroix, among many others. What catches my eye are two plaintive, yet hauntingly beautiful, paintings of Mary Magdalene, one by Francesco Albani. It seems the duke was interested in the Magdalene too. We also find the Reading Room and library quite interesting, with its important collection of medieval manuscripts and brightly colored, intricate illustrations.

We have a late lunch at the château at La Capitainerie just before it closes for the day. We will have to wait to order that Chantilly cake and berries if we are ever fortunate enough to return here. Then, we are hurriedly off. We have missed the last bus back to the city central, but this allows us a lovely, guided walk, or should I say run, through a long grove of trees to eventually reach the train station for our return to Paris.

Painted from *Our Lady of Perpetual Help*

Walking West on the Camino—on the Vézelay Route 57

Painted from Georges de la Tour's *The Penitent Magdalen*

Ah belle Paris—au revoir! As we prepare to board Air France for our return to the States, I am already plotting my return to the Camino next summer and to our further adventures on the Vézelay Route.

II.
Spring 2020 to Summer 2022
The Valley of Tears

*To everything there is a season, and a time to every
purpose under heaven. Ecclesiastes 3:1*

In March of 2020, the world stopped. No thanks to the Covid-19 pandemic, what should have been a happy time of anticipation for returning to the Vézelay Route in the spring gave way to an eerie silent standstill. We were all sent home to shelter in place, at least those of us fortunate enough to be able to work at home. The courts closed. My days consisted of endless meetings, phone calls, emails, foster home visits, and hearings all accomplished remotely by Zoom. For my part, my only personal outing was to venture across town to pick up my groceries outside Walmart very early on certain Sundays. I considered it a treat. Others were not so lucky; people were dying, especially the most vulnerable—the elderly, frontline workers, and those with underlying health conditions. A black plague had descended upon us in modern times.

Little was understood about the virus. My walks to vespers every evening at the Carmelite Monastery turned into regular treks to sit instead on a concrete slab under my favorite crabapple tree, which stands gracefully right outside the chapel door. She embraced me, *Madame Pommiere a Crabe*, as she waved her arms toward heaven and swayed gently to the melodies of the nuns cloistered inside. The sacred songs and prayers waft out the open window into the gentle breeze of nightfall, mixing with the birdsong, and then to our listening ears. I hug my tree almost every day. She stands resolute and strong, and, most importantly, silent. There is much to be learned from her resilience as she bends to the seasons and to the winds of change but does not break. I wonder if she has learned from me too in some way simply because I sit with her in the silence of nature. *Moi*, her pilgrim friend. It was fall by now; the leaves were turning a glittering gold and brilliant red. As I sat under the tree, I looked out over the horizon and found comfort in the quietude. Soon the collective cold of winter will fall on the land. I could feel it in the air.

By the spring of 2021, I was making plans to retire and to move east to live with my sister Marcia, a move anticipated for a long time. I was excited. The crabapple tree was sporting her new Easter outfit of bright pink petals. Hope was in the air and, especially, that the pandemic might be waning. Without recounting my sad story encore une fois here, let's just say I moved, but my household belongings, my mother's antiques, my books, and art never arrived. I lost everything. That medieval story comes to mind of early pilgrims on the Camino who were robbed by bandits on the banks of a certain deep and murky river in Spain—only, the modern tale is that of unsuspecting folks who lost everything in moving scams. I have come to realize that the rain falls on everyone. If and how you get back up from the obstacles on your path is the larger question.

I did all I could to remedy the situation, and I still hope to this day that I might receive a phone call from a Good Samaritan that some of my things have been located. Unable to really settle in with my sister, I returned to Santa Fe two months later with my cat in tow. However, the universe wasn't done with me yet by divine design or otherwise. My SUV died; my Seiko watch of thirty years broke and was unrepairable; my rent at the same unit increased substantially; and I ended up in the emergency room passing kidney stones the second night I was back.

The great Spanish, medieval mystic and counterpart to St. Teresa of Avila, Saint John of the Cross, might call this "the dark night of the soul." It is most certainly a dissolution of self. I had prayed for the death of my ego months before as I was retiring from the practice of law. Now I pray simply for the strength to get up off the ground. *Ça suffit!* And eight months after returning to Santa Fe, my little cat Grayson died, no matter my best efforts to help him. The cycle of life was complete. I could barely pick myself up out of the dirt. A wise one told me it was all okay because I was growing new roots, a thing I have so much admired in my crabby apple tree. *Mme. Pommiere a Crabe* has large mounds of roots piled at her base which, I suspect, fan outward underground at great lengths. Her main action is underground, and so might mine be also at this stage of my life, in the dark recesses of the earth. It is quite refreshing in an odd sort of way, to be divested of everything and stripped to the bone. Make no mistake, my tears could fill an ocean. I am reminded of what Mother Superior Marie Bernadette from the monastery told me one time, something about this world was "the valley of tears". And so it is. But, maybe, I am the fortunate one since I have not endured the pain of losing a close loved one to covid as so many others have. Detachment, for me, is the order of the day. I am still working on it. Admittedly, I was forced into this release of ego and all I knew and possessed, unlike James and John, who dropped their fishing nets willingly and followed Jesus, unfettered and with great faith.

Saint John of the Cross wrote of "the dark night" in the context of his early dry and barren meditations and of his inner life. But couldn't "the dark night" also refer to our own outer struggles in the world? Maybe they are one and the same. St.

John wrote, "The endurance of darkness is preparation for great light." I hope he's right.

The seasons turn, but divine order is at play amid the seeming chaos. As I was drifting off to sleep late one night on another winter's icy eve, I was jarred back into a waking state by a shimmering half-moon that had pierced the edges of my curtains and kissed me goodnight. As I drifted back to sleep, I felt myself transported into the heavens for a brief rendezvous with my college sweetheart from long ago, now deceased. Was it a lucid dream? All I know is that I felt a sweet embrace and encouragement to press on.

It is late summer of 2022. Bright crimson crabapples hang from *Madame's* verdant, leafy-green branches. I am making plans to resume my walk on the Vézelay Route *seule*. That's right—alone. Marcia is unable to go with me due to a recent nasty bout of Rocky Mountain spotted fever from a tick bite. She has had her own "dark night". I have managed to replenish my hiking supplies from resale shops and to purchase a new backpack on sale from REI. Is someone out there enjoying my old backpack, I wonder, that one with all those colorful Camino patches lovingly sewn in a line down the back. It is hard sometimes not to feel some amount of sorrow and resentment still over my things that were lost and not returned. Apparently, I have more release work to do as I walk my pilgrimage once more, including letting go of past regrets and traumas. I remind myself I am here for a reason and that I must have chosen these obstacles at my life review for lessons learned, so you best get on with it, *mon amie!*

Might I be on a fool's errand, like the Fool in the Tarot? The fool jumps off the cliff with abandon, her knapsack tied to a pole flung across her shoulder. I am trading despair and fear for faith. But not so fast. Fear thoughts have come marching up in mass clamoring for my attention. What about the pandemic, and will I be safe in September mixing with other people on trains, buses, and airplanes? What about hiking alone and if I fall and break a leg out in the middle of nowhere? What if I step on a snake in the

Walking West on the Camino—on the Vézelay Route

Autumn Stillness under the Crabapple Tree

Chill of Winter at the Carmelite Monastery

Au Printemps—Hope for a New Day

Summer of 2022—The Camino Calls

Walking West on the Camino—on the Vézelay Route

weeds and grass by the murky waters of the old Canal du Berry? So it went. And what happens next might just be a cautionary tale.

One lovely late summer afternoon soon after, as I was making my way through dense brush to my favorite apricot tree up at the monastery, my little world of imaginary fears came crashing in around me. I just happened to look down and stop dead in my tracks. A large snake was sprawled across my path not two feet away. It had managed, somehow, to emerge from my imagination into my reality. The law of attraction, I guess. That which you fear comes upon you. Or I could blame it, not on my errant thoughts, but on coincidence, although I know full well nothing much happens 'by accident". Well, at least I didn't step on it, I tell myself, as I walk back home, shaken.

My new self-talk is of little comfort tonight as I try to drift off to sleep. That snake has slithered into my head, and every time I close my eyes, there it is. I usually don't have obsessive, fear-based thoughts, until now. But as I lie here, fresh new thoughts come to me which are of great comfort. Years ago, I painted Rubens' the Immaculate Conception. The Blessed Mary is standing on a globe trampling a serpent. And before I could fully process that image, another one appears. That ole snake is shedding its skin to make way for something new. Okay, so I like these images better, and I fall into a deep and restful sleep. The Camino is once again whispering my name and perhaps yours too. Listen, can you hear it?

La Vie en Rose—Seeing life through rose-colored glasses

III.
Fall 2022
Nevers to Saint-Jean-Pied-de-Port

150 MILES—30 DAYS

Nevers, Cuffy, Sancoins, La Croix, Charenton-du-Cher, Saint-Amand Montrond, La Souterraine, Bénévent l'Abbaye, St. Léonard-de-Noblat, Limoges, Aixe-sur-Vienne, La Coquille, Thiviers, Périgueux, Saint-Astier, Mussidan, La Gratade, Chateau Puy Servain, Saint-Foy-la-Grande, Mont-de-Marsan, Saint-Sever, Hagetmau, Sault-de-Navailles, Orthez, Saint-Jean-Pied-de-Port

Surely goodness and mercy shall follow me all the days of my life...Psalm 23:6

The winds of change have arranged it so that I am setting out in September, alone. My good friends from Houston are staying at my home in Santa Fe and will be hiking a lot and feeding my two outdoor cats. I have left my car at a long-term parking lot in Albuquerque. The flight from Albuquerque to Atlanta has gone well, and after a wait of several hours in the Atlanta Airport, I am now in transit to the *Paris Charles de*

Gaulle Aéroport. I am hoping the French I have studied for years with Pimsleur will kick in once we land. With little sleep, all those French phrases are a jumble in my head, and, of course, all my meticulous French study notes were lost in the moving scam, along with everything else. I have switched to Duolingo online. That was then, and this is now, I remind myself. There is hope ahead.

Via the local RER B train from the Charles de Gaulle station to Châtelet-Les Halles, then a convoluted walk to the metro stop at Châtelet, then the metro to Bercy, then another walk to the *Paris Gare de Bercy*, then a wait for a few hours at the train station there, then a SNCF two-hour regional train, I finally reach Nevers, my starting point this year on the Vézelay Route. I might have been tempted to stay in bed had I known what was in store for me today. Once in Nevers, I follow the street signs for *la centre ville* and wind my way through cobblestone streets until I finally reach the *Espace Bernadette Soubirous* where I have booked a room for the night. I present my new pilgrim passport which I had ordered from the Association of American Pilgrims before I left home. I have copied Marcia's pilgrim stamps from our walk from Vézelay to Nevers in 2019 into my new credential. For the pilgrim rate of twenty-five euros, I have a simple room which overlooks the loveliest interior courtyard at the convent, as well as *le petit déjeuner* for tomorrow morning. I pay a visit once more to Saint Bernadette of Lourdes whose incorrupt body lies in a crystal reliquary at the altar of a side chapel. The silence is golden. By now, I have all but forgotten my long, frenzied day spent getting here, fortunate me.

Baguettes, croissants, muesli, yogurt, an assortment of homemade jams, butter, steaming hot cafe au lait await us on the breakfast tables for our *petit déjeuner*. A friendly woman from Brussels has joined me; she just completed a bike ride on the Vézelay Route for a week with one of her friends, and she is driving back to Belgium this morning. I can't help but notice that no one else seems to be walking the Camino today, *seulement moi*. After some time spent at the garden shrine for St. Bernadette, I take up my backpack and head down Rue Saint-Gildard leaving town. My walking guide, courtesy of the Dutch Confraternity of Saint James, takes me by the *Cathédrale Saint Cyr-Sainte Julitte*. The church, from both the fourteenth-century Gothic and the older Romanesque period, is open, much to my delight.

Saint Cyricus and his mother, Julitta, were early Christian martyrs who were executed at Tarsus in the early fourth century. Saint Cyr is venerated in churches around the world, but especially at the Nevers Cathedral where some of his purported relics are kept. The spectacular, high, rounded arches and vaults in the nave glow gold and pink in the dim light amid colorful, old stained-glass windows. A beautiful contemporary stained-glass window, in shades of blue and white, graces a small side chamber. I sit in awe for a while taking it all in, but then, I am up and out for I have a long way to go this day. Well, long enough for me. I am headed for the small village of Cuffy, a little over seven miles away, enough for my first day back on the Camino. Before I left for France, I managed to reserve a room, dinner, and *le petit déjeuner* for fifty euros, the pilgrim rate, at *La Grenouille*, a small hotel and restaurant on the Dutch Confraternity's list of suggested accommodations.

I am taking the slightly shorter Augy variant route on the GR 654. Leaving Nevers, I head down *Rue de la Cathédrale* past the old eighteenth-century Bishop's Palace, the *Place du Palais*, and cross the long bridge over the Loire River. Dark clouds are gathering.

By lunchtime, I find myself sitting on a curb having leftover slices of baguettes and fresh strawberry jam, huddled under my plastic cape, in the drizzling rain. Sooner or later, really, much later, I reach that railroad bridge described in my guide and pass the cemetery, also described. Then, I wind back and forth on a cycle path along a canal and finally walk through the hamlet of Gimouille. Much of the route is on narrow asphalt lanes and pleasant, grassy dirt roads. The rain has stopped. Walking alone is a big adjustment for me and a little unsettling. The trees, their leaves rustling in the breeze, and the birds are my only companions. We are eventually welcomed by bright red geraniums in window boxes placed on iron railings on both sides of the road leading into Cuffy.

La Grenouille, literally "the frog", is located at the entrance to Cuffy. Frog décor is everywhere, not to mention that huge, dark-green frog plastered high on the side of the hotel between cheery red awnings and shutters. The bar and restaurant are busy this late Saturday afternoon preparing for wedding festivities tonight. I am glad I booked early. Despite the hustle and bustle, their hospitality toward me is impressive; even Chef Gilbert has emerged from the kitchen, with an easy manner, to help translate.

At *le diner*, I am seated at one of the small tables in the bar area next to a table with, to my amazement, *another pilgrim*. Pilgrim Danni has walked from his home in Belgium and is headed to Santiago de Compostela at the far northwestern reaches of Spain. Some friends of his, pilgrims from the past, have joined him here for dinner. I am another old friend to them, we who excitedly struggle to understand each other in broken French, English, and German. Our pilgrim supper consists of fish and chips, a salad, cheese, coconut ice cream with red wine and wonderful French baguettes. The specialty of the house, frog legs with parsley (of course) is happily not offered on our pilgrim menu. Yikes!

I have retraced my steps after leaving La Grenouille to rejoin the Vézelay Route on the cycle path along a canal just to the left of the hotel. The air is crisp, and the sky is bright blue this early morning. I had hoped to reach the pilgrim hostel at La Croix today, but I soon see that I must call ahead and reserve a space for tomorrow night instead. As it is, if I reach Sancoins, which is before La Croix, I will have already walked almost fifteen miles. After passing under a railroad bridge, I am directed onto an asphalt road toward the small village of Apremont-sur-Allier.

To my good fortune, the church in Apremont-sur-Allier is open. *Notre Dame de l'Assomption* dates to 1861; it was built on the remains of the older Romanesque church here. A beautiful blue, stained-glass window inside depicts Saint-Roch, the pilgrim, with his staff and gourd, his dog at his side. I sit for a while under the old chandelier at the altar and then go on.

My walking guide, as well as the blue and yellow pilgrim markers on trees, sends me "through the forest", then past the hamlet of Les Coqs and behind the castle at *Grossouvre*. I have been in the wilds most of this day. My emergence out into semi-open spaces to start on the grassy footpath beside the murky, green waters of the old *Canal du Berry* is less than encouraging. By now, I have put on my tall hiking (serpent) gaiters just for my own peace of mind, if there is any at this point. The Canal du Berry, once a vibrant commercial canal along the Loire, is overgrown with tall grasses and scrubs. I am walking on one side of it, and then must cross at various bridges and walk the other side; it goes on endlessly. At this point, I sit down on the ground for a rest, in a mini-meltdown, exhausted and unhappy that this portion of the Camino is so long and so hard. At the bridge of *Sancoins*, I turn an abrupt, desperate left off the canal and walk through the residential area for almost two miles and finally reach the *centre ville* of Sancoins. I don't have reservations here although I had tried to book something before I left home, without success. Pilgrim Danni told me that he had booked at the Hotel Saint-Joseph, but they never returned my emails.

I have dragged myself, hot and sweaty and almost out of water, over to the lovely Saint-Joseph, eighteen miles for today's little walk. I can secure a room here, *le diner*, and *le petit déjeuner*. Thank God, or I might have found myself sleeping out under the stars tonight. Suddenly, the romance of the Milky Way seems like a little much. Revived, after a hot shower and a nap, I have dinner outside in the hotel's back patio under a canopy of trees. *Le poisson, une salade verte, des frites, du pain, un verre de vin rouge, des fromages, et crème brulée for le dessert—un diner* fit for a queen. *N'est-ce pas!*

After *le petit déjeuner* at the hotel, I retrace my steps out of Sancoins and eventually reach the towpath along the Canal du Berry and turn left to pick up where I left off yesterday. Pilgrim Danni had stopped at a *pâtisserie* for *croissants au chocolat,* but now, because he walks much faster than I do, passes me with a nod and disappears down the path, despite my best efforts to keep him in sight. The cool of the morning has given way to a blazing hot sun by early afternoon. My guidebook wisely recommends staying on the side of the canal that offers shade, and yet I am also sent on bridges back and forth across the canal, sometimes into shade, but now into a very long stretch of sunshine on the right bank. As we already know, the Canal du Berry stretches on for what seems like forever, in the wilds. I find myself straining my eyes to make out what exactly that large, dark object way in the distance in front of me might be. I can go back, or I can go forward. Either way is a long way to walk. I eventually realize that I am approaching a lone car parked on the narrow towpath between the canal and the dense underbrush and trees. As I pass by, I see a young muscular man, his shirt off, full of tattoos, sitting there—no fishing poles set out and no acknowledgement as I walk by, no nothing. He had driven up that narrow towpath and was just sitting there sweating in his car in the heat of the day. And so, too, am I, because as soon as I disappear behind a curve, I start to run, praying all the way. Several more miles, and I am directed left onto the Arnon bridge and then off the canal. And who should I see sitting there resting and adjusting his boots on the left bank but my *nouveau ami,* Pilgrim Danni. Together, we walk down a small, paved road toward the *Domaine de Bellevue.* And so goes my adventures along the old Canal du Berry on the *Voie de Vézelay.* I live to tell the tale.

The *Domaine de Bellevue* is an ancient farmhouse and surrounding buildings that sits at the top of the road amid fields and fields of sunflowers. The sunflowers have since bloomed and gone to seed, but their dormant beauty persists. Pilgrim Danni has walked on, and I have dropped my backpack for a brief nap under the sheltering, shady arms of a walnut tree just across the road. But soon enough, I walk on toward the pilgrim hostel, Nos Repos, which is in the small hamlet of La Croix. Friendly *hospitaliers* are awaiting my arrival; Pilgrim Danni has already showered and unpacked and claimed his little bed in a large rustic dormitory room up a long flight of stairs. I take a bed in a side chamber under the eaves. These volunteers are an x-pilgrim couple who drive down from Holland for a few weeks every year to help at the *gite*. They have a separate apartment on the property right across from the chicken coup and henhouse. The whistling wind and gathering black clouds have forced us to take shelter inside for our early supper, just in the nick of time. Just before *le diner*, the sky proceeds to dump buckets of rain and hail in the outdoor picnic area and patio. By candlelight, now that we have lost electricity, we hear the saga of that rooster out with the hens, who has lost his tail feathers. It seems that the previous *hospitaliers* had let the chickens and rooster out to run free for a day, but only the hens returned to their pen by nightfall. That ole rooster had to be chased down and corralled in a fenced area to get him safely home that night, at the expense of his tail feathers, in the ensuing chaos. "Do tail feathers grow back?" I ask. Everyone just looks at me. It has been a long day, and we all escape to our beds for a good night's sleep.

After *le petit déjeuner,* we are again out early. Our *hospitaliers* have helped me call ahead to Mme. Mativon to reserve a pilgrim bed and meals. Mme. Mativon has long opened her lovely home to pilgrims passing through the village of Charenton-du-Cher on their way west on the Vézelay Route. I had tried to book with her before I left home, but my e-mails had gone unanswered. I had assumed she was no longer taking pilgrims, but Pilgrim Danni has already reserved there for tonight. The Camino

Along the Canal du Berry

seems to have provided Pilgrim Danni lately to be my trusty compass for where I might stay next. I am calling ahead on this trip because some refuges have closed due to an inability to keep their facilities open because of a scarcity of pilgrims during the pandemic. I have also read on pilgrim association websites that some of the larger communal gites in France are offering beds to refugees from Ukraine and have closed their doors to pilgrims.

Pilgrim Danni has long since passed me by this morning, but I am not deterred. I have eleven miles to walk today, and I see that my old friend, the Canal du Berry, is awaiting my return. I am taking another shortcut variant, this time, via the Bridge of Vernais along the canal. The gites at both Augy-Sur-Aubois and at Ainay-le-Chateau. are closed, so I am heading straight to Charenton-du-Cher. My path takes me through dense woods for miles and eventually through the hamlets of Les Brusques and later, Laugere. I stop to have a rest and *le déjeuner* (an energy bar and water) at a picnic table; a bull is grazing in his pasture just behind me, barely looking up. That's good. Soon enough, I am walking the towpath again along the canal and pass several locks until I am finally directed to the left off the canal and down Rue du Stade toward Charenton-du-Cher. I have an address for Mme. Mativon's home, but my GPS sends me on a wild goose chase through the *ville*. I have managed to find a small market and have replenished my supplies, just as a deluge of rain quickly passes through. Serendipitously, Madame's home is just a block away.

As it turns out, Madame Mativon's daughter has moved in with her mother and is helping to renovate and upgrade the home and gardens. Mme. Mativon is recuperating in a rehabilitation center after a fall. Pilgrim Danni and I sit at the kitchen table with the younger Mme. and her boyfriend for an early supper, complete with a homemade apple tart for dessert, along with local cheeses. My cozy *chambre*, furnished with beautiful antiques, has two single beds. I have collapsed into one of them, ready to call it a day.

Today's journey takes me down narrow asphalt roads leaving town, then past a cemetery, an electrical facility, through dense woods, and to the hamlet of Saint-Pierre-les-Etieux. At the *Moulin de Gateau*, a beautiful old bed and breakfast, I am joined by two large fluffy, friendly dogs who walk with me a long way on a path through the woods, until I can shake them and walk on alone. I hope to reach the city of Saint-Amand-Montrond today, seven and a half miles. Pilgrim Danni has walked on, but not before recommending that I stay at the youth hostel in Saint-Amand; all the other gites are closed. By the time I reach the *Foyer des Jeunes Travailleurs* in St. Amand, I have walked an extra three miles across town. But once here, I have a clean private room for twenty-five euros. There are very few others staying here. I have reserved breakfast and then walk several blocks to a Carrefour for tomorrow's pilgrim supplies and something for dinner in my room. *Pas de probleme!*

My trek across Saint-Armand has positioned me within several miles, walking distance, of the *gare*, a train station relatively nearby. *Les gares* are few and far between, and today, I am taking advantage of it. A truly lightbulb moment has gone off in my head, one might say. I have roughly only thirty days in France to walk the Vézelay Route and reach Saint-Jean-Pied-de-Port, the end point on my trip. My pilgrimage, *my way*, means walking and now riding the train; otherwise, I will never get to my destination in the time I have allotted. Happily, I arrive several hours later *en train* to the next *la gare* on the Camino, in the medieval village of La Souterraine. I have managed to call ahead and book a room at Hotel Jinjaud, a small hotel in the *centre ville* which is on the list of accommodations published by the Dutch Confraternity. Today, my GPS does not disappoint, and I eventually locate the hotel at 4 Rue de Limoges. The Camino has outdone itself in arranging my stay here. The old, family-run Restaurant-Bar-Hotel Jinjaud, open since 1951 and recently renovated, is the picture of charm and easy hospitality. Its distinctive, dark wood exterior is set against silver stone and large, white, shuttered windows. I am shown to my little upstairs room, which I immediately realize I might never want to leave. I am in "the green room:" glittery, swirled, light-green wallpaper; a dark-green velvet antique chair, table, and armoire; a floral chandelier amid exposed wooden beams; and small windows under the eaves that overlook walls of cascading ivy set in a small courtyard. My favorite Disney princess movies never prepared me for this. A seventy-one-year-old lone pilgrim, who stumbled in with her heavy rucksack seconds ago, now finds herself resting her weary head on her bed under a *magnifique*, little, green canopy, Mademoiselle Moi.

There are three other guests at dinner, including a friendly Flemish pilgrim from Belgium who speaks some English. On lovely bright pink tablecloths, we are served the regional specialty of *Limousin* beef, along with a traditional *salade niçoise*, French baguettes, *vin rouge, fromage, et crème brulée*. I have returned to my room, thinking I might prolong my stay here for another night, I love it so much.

This morning, however, after a *petit déjeuner* of sliced baguettes, croissants, homemade jam and butter, and yogurt, I hastily returned to my room and pack up to leave. The Camino is a flow, and I must place myself in it and press on. My destination today is the hamlet of Bénévent-l'Abbaye, thirteen miles away. I found *Les Ramparts* on booking.com and have reserved for tonight. It is a relief; most gites have closed in this area. My guidebook sends me in front of the church and then by *Place du Marché*, straight ahead under the *Porte Saint Jean*, and then onto *Rue Saint Jacques* for a long stretch across La Souterrainne. After crossing over a railway bridge, then passing under a tunnel on a footpath, I pick up walking by the busy, narrow D10 through hamlets, including Saint-Priest-la-Feuille. *L'Eglise Saint Laurent*, the beautiful old church at Saint-Priest, is open, and I sit for some time in its cool

Just Past La Souterraine

Walking West on the Camino—on the Vézelay Route 81

interior. By now, the Belgian pilgrim I met last night has caught up with me, along with a young man from France. Together we walk for miles until the young Frenchman leaves us to look for a refuge for the night. He is a new pilgrim, and his pack is so large and heavy that he can barely stand up. He will need to unload some of his burdens soon, grow stronger, or simply leave the Camino altogether. The Camino has a way of working such things out. Walking now through the village of Chamborand, we stop to visit a lovely, old church here. Fortunately for us, we have lost our way somewhere in the countryside past a dam and meander unwittingly down and around narrow asphalt roads until we reach the D10 again. But this affords us a direct route straight to Bénévent-l'Abbaye. Dark clouds are gathering, and the cold rain comes just as we reach the *Hotel-Restaurant Les Ramparts.*

Les Ramparts, a perfect oasis for this night, is owned and operated by an Englishman, Dan Allen, and his French partner, Francoise. I am situated in their "purple room" with its boa-feather purple pillows strewn on the bed and purple artwork on purple walls. What has the Camino arranged for me? I never liked purple much, until now. It is all so charming and fun. At dinner, I am seated with my fellow pilgrim from Belgium. We both order from the pilgrim menu: quiche, fish and chips, fresh salad, vin rouge, baguettes, and *gateau au citron* for dessert. It is all superb. My fellow pilgrim explains, over his second glass of wine (not mine), that he had purposely slowed his walking pace to match mine today to pursue some sort of dalliance this evening with me. He tells me that all married European men have affairs and that I was missing out on a good time. He is growing more insistent and a little scary, and with that, I politely say good night. Now, happily, up in my room *seule*, I sink into my boa pillows and fall fast asleep, unperturbed. I walk the Camino to unload unnecessary baggage, not to create more, even fleetingly. I have also heard every line in the book at this age.

After a very early *petit déjeuner*, Francoise graciously gives me a ride to the next rail station, at Marsac, only three miles away. I am taking the train this morning to Saint-Léonard de Noblat via a complicated train schedule of various stops, train changes, and waits. *Saint-Léonard* is a small town, but it takes me over an hour to walk approximately four miles into the old section around the church. I wind up shady, cobbled streets and by a large walled park that stretches on and on. The Romanesque *Collégiale Eglise de Saint-Léonard de Noblat* has been listed as a UNESCO World Heritage Site since1998. Saint Leonard, a Frankish nobleman at the court of Clovis in the mid-first century, renounced all for the Benedictine order. Legend has it that he convinced King Clovis to allow him to release prisoners from time to time that he deemed to be worthy. He later became a hermit-monk in the forests in the *Limousin*, part of an ancient region that is now known as the *Nouvelle Aquitaine*. In 1438, King Charles VII of France traveled to the old abbey which Leonard had founded in Noblat and venerated St. Leonard's remains there. The Abbey of Noblat and Saint Leonard's tomb thus became a popular cult stop on the Vézelay Route, especially promoted by the *Codex Calixtinus*. Not surprisingly, across Europe, Saint Leonard is the patron saint of prisoners.

I must see the church before I arrange a place to sleep. The *Eglise de Saint-Léonard* is a massive stone structure of high vaults and pillars. Large circular, silver chandeliers hang in a row down the ceiling of the dark nave. The golden tomb of Saint Leonard sits high behind the front altar with a blue crest of three *fleurs-de-lis* hanging above it. The symbol of leg irons and chains is also prevalent on the crest as well as on an iron crate in a side chamber. The *fleur de lys*, which literally means 'flower of the lily', is strongly linked to King Clovis and his conversion to Christianity. A three-pointed, golden yellow iris is said to have miraculously appeared on the King's coat of arms and shield in battle. A symbol of the Trinity, the *fleur de lys* established its

Walking West on the Camino—on the Vézelay Route 83

place in history. It can be found in churches and chateaus across Europe, especially in France, now heralding royalty. I am also interested in a large, beautiful, old painting of a group of both men and women huddled below the cross at the crucifixion, one scantily clad female I believe to be depicting Mary Magdalene. Those old tales of the Magdalene as a prostitute regrettably remain, it seems, to this day.

As I again emerge into the bright sunlight, I am on a mission to get to the *Office de Tourisme* before it closes at five. According to my list of accommodations, I must reserve and pick up a key at the tourist office to stay at the municipal gite run by the Amis de Saint Jacques. I am afraid, however, that my GPS has sent me on the scenic route through the winding streets of the old section of town. I stand, finally, at its door gazing at it as if it were a mirage. I pay the fee of fifteen euros and return to the church; the gite is located right across the street in another massive, stone building. This gite is quite spartan, even for me, and since I would most likely be the only one there, I race back to the tourist office to return the key and to get a refund, now making myself a complete annoyance to the poor woman behind the desk. She points me up the street toward a hotel which might take pilgrims at a reduced rate. But do I care at this point, this spoiled pilgrim! I have soon settled in at the *Hotel et Restaurant Relais de Saint Jacques* which, as it turns out, is also on my list. For seventy euros, the pilgrim rate, I have booked a lovely little room, *le diner, et le petit déjeuner*. I contact my sister every night by Facebook Messenger, and tonight, we both revel in my good fortune.

This morning, I make my way back across town to the train station It is Sunday morning, and the *gare* is closed. But I had managed to study my schedule yesterday and to plan ahead. I had purchased a ticket for Limoges which is an hour away by rail. The beautiful city of Limoges is another major pilgrim halt on the Vézelay Route, and I want to see it. By the time I get to Limoges and walk to the old part of town, about three miles, it is almost noon. I have managed to find the cathedral first off, which sits at *2 Rue Neuve Saint-Etienne*. The *Cathédrale-Saint-Etienne de Limoges* beautifully depicts both Romanesque and Gothic, as well as Renaissance architectural styles. Its looming, octagonal belltower comes into full view against the bright blue sky as I round a line of trees down a narrow-cobbled street to reach it. Work on this church dedicated to St. Stephen and later, Bishop Jean de Langeac, began in 1273. It is a national monument. I see why when I go inside. Colorful frescoes of some of the saints and Jesus in majesty stand stately behind the main alter. Looking up at the domed ceiling, I can't help but gaze in awe at the majestic field of golden, twinkling stars on azure blue with touches of crimson. Medieval paintings line the walls. I rest for some time in the cool of its massive stone womb, reluctant to go on.

Once outside, I am caught up in the excitement of an antique market set up under umbrellas in the streets surrounding the cathedral. So much fun, especially for this pilgrim who is painfully mindful throughout that anything she buys will have to be schlepped home on her back. But, of course, that, apparently, isn't much of a deterrence since I have found tourist trinkets for both me and my sister, a lovely little hand-painted Limoges porcelain bowl and a small gold mirror in the French style. I discovered later, with research online, that I have purchased a Limoges Fragonard Courting Couple vintage vanity dish for nine euros, such a delight!

My next destination is the *Musée National Adrien Dubouché* at Place Winston Churchill, the museum displaying the history and old masterpieces of Limoges porcelain. My GPS gets me over there, several miles across town, but only with some back-and-forth effort on my part. I am lucky it is open today and hurry in, glad to drop my added load at the door. Beginning in the late-eighteenth century, what was known as hard-paste porcelain factories sprang up in areas around Limoges, due to the clay mined in that area used for the porcelain. One striking, modern-art display is that of plates hand-painted in gold and white arranged in a cross representing the crucifixion. Gorgeous, colorful porcelain bowls, plates, clocks, statuary in all types, modern and classic old French patterns, are displayed on four floors. I am here for almost two hours, but by now, I am becoming mindful of the time, and I still must locate my *gite* for the night.

I have my late-afternoon lunch of leftover baguettes and cheese on a bench under some trees in the museum gardens. I then turn on my GPS again for about a five-mile walk across town, up long hills and through questionable areas of local commerce, until I finally reach my refuge in a peaceful, quiet part of the city at 33 Rue Charlemagne. I have booked a room and *le petit déjeuner* with Mme. Marie-Reine Jouanin, whose *chambre d'hote* is on my list of accommodations published by the Dutch Confraternity. Madame. Jouanin is quite accommodating and helpful, and her own charming artwork is on display in her kitchen. I have a private little comfortable bedroom and bath in her home, separate from her living quarters upstairs. I am happy later to stretch across my bed and call my sister. Such a full day as this on the Camino and off must be reported, especially the fact that I have a mystery gift I will be bringing her back from France. My sore, aching feet and toes have reminded me to let go now and drift into restful sleep. This, my last mission of the day, is accomplished.

I have gotten explicit written instructions on how to catch the city bus near Mme. Jouanin's home and to then change buses correctly leaving Limoges to intersect with the Vézelay Route several miles out of the *centre ville*. However, the bus driver, looking perplexed, drops me off near the hospital, and I am left to bug the next bus driver who happens by to help me. She, with a kindly older woman on board, determine where I should be let off again. After much excited conversation between them in French and pointing and profuse "*merci beaucoups*" on my part, I eventually find myself walking a diagonal dirt path up a grassy hill to the Camino signs for the Vézelay Route. I am relieved to

Marché de Rue—in Limoges

see them as if I have found my way home once more. But now, I am walking miles through the outer reaches of Limoges and then through residential suburbs stretching out for several more miles. My destination today is almost ten miles away, Aixe-sur-Vienne. I have reserved another *chambre d'hote* online.

The route takes me toward the village of Merignac, through roundabouts in congested areas, then on a long grassy path through the forest. I cross the bridge over the Vienne River and then the Aixette. At the entrance to Aixe-sur-Vienne, I turn left by the church (closed) onto *Rue Victor Hugo* and end up, fairly turned around, on *Avenue du Président Wilson* at a *boulangerie*. I stop here for *un grand biscuit et un café au lait*. The Camino, it seems, is serving cookies and coffee this late afternoon in a lovely little bakery. By the time I continue past the town and up into the hills of a residential area to the bed and breakfast, on *All. le Grand Rieux*, I have walked three more miles in the hot sun. I'm not complaining as much as I'm just saying. I am exhausted, and my toes feel like throbbing appendages in my boots. Well, now I'm complaining...sorry.

Madame Veronique Pain and her husband, Gérard, are gracious hosts and wonderful cooks. We sit at their table for a five-course meal: tomatoes from their garden with fresh herbs; gazpacho; fish cakes with steamed millet; *une tarte aux pommes*; scrumptious local fresh fromage; French baguettes, and red wine. *Monsieur Gérard* and I banter back and forth at dinner in his bad English and my bad French with gusto. Any complaints about my journey today are long forgotten. Except, regrettably, they are still recorded in concrete in the Book of Life or Akashic Record, I suppose. I have a comfortable room and private bath. Sleep comes quickly.

⚜

After *le petit déjeuner, Monsieur Gérard* has kindly driven me back across the *Vienne* to the *gare*. I am taking the train to the small village of La Coquille this morning. *Gérard* also helped me call ahead to the *Refuge Pelerins,* run by the *Amis de Saint Jacque*, in La Coquille. The *gites* operated by the pilgrim associations do not take reservations since they are on a first come, first served basis, but they do want a courtesy call, if possible, to be able to plan for meals. For twenty-five euros, I now have a bed, *le diner*, and *le petit déjeuner*. I am relieved. The story goes that the village of La Coquille got its name from its early tradition of giving a scallop shell to those pilgrims who passed through its parish on their way west to Santiago de Compostela. La Coquille sits in the *Dordogne Department of* southwestern France, also known as the *Périgord*. The region is known for its truffles, its chalk cliffs and quarries, for its wine industry, and most importantly, for its lush forests and wildlife. After all the local stops, I arrive in La Coquille in under two hours. It can be a simple pleasure to ride the French rail system most days, and today is no exception. Heavy rains are predicted, and soon enough, the drizzle of rain begins to stream down my windowpane. The train is crowded, and bikers have hung their *velos* next to the exits. Once in La Coquille, I follow the signs for the *centre ville* and walk about three miles into the village and, finally, to the *Refuge Pelerins, Impasse Saint Jean*. The rain is dripping off my nose, down my slick hiking pants, and into my soggy boots. The *hospitalier* has agreed to let me check in early today. The outside of the *gite* is painted in wild colors and graffiti designed just for us pilgrims in mind. *Jean* is busy cooking and preparing chicken and fresh vegetables for our dinner tonight. He is expecting two others, and, before long, we are all there showering and arranging our tiny beds and blankets for tonight. *Jean* has a small private room by the kitchen. The *gite* accommodates six pilgrims in one large dormitory room. The older French couple who has arrived speak very little English, but they also see I am trying to speak French, so we have adjusted amiably together. The Frenchman has walked the Camino before, but he wants his wife to experience it now with him. One might laugh and add, "*la misere aime souvent la compagnie,*" especially on a wet, cold day like today. But, finding out that the old church is open, I retrace my steps back to the village, and sit in its cool solitude for quite some time.

Walking West on the Camino—on the Vézelay Route 89

Café au lait and toasted baguettes with fresh butter and homemade blackberry jam lighten our spirits this morning, although the continuing cold rain serves as a reminder for me to put on my high hiking gaiters and my raincape. Fortunately, *Jean*, our *hospitalier*, has allowed me to stay later until it is predicted when the rain will stop, about ten o'clock this morning. As the sun is ever so tentatively peeking out from under the clouds, I turn right at the main road by the *gite* and catch the Vézelay Route and the Camino waymarks once more. I am headed for the city of Thiviers, twelve miles away. I have booked online with *Madame Cordier* at *Les Conches*, another *chambre d'hotes* on my list of pilgrim accommodations. *Mme.* wants me there only after four p.m. Not a problem since I have a long way to go; I will be most happy to get there before dark.

My map has me first descending to the hamlet of *Moulin de Margaud* and then ascending to Les Rivailles. Yes, up and up I go on a narrow asphalt road that has now become a dirt road. At the top, I am sent on a path seemingly stretching on forever "across the plateau…and through forests and fields." Finally, past the hamlet of *Pont Fermier* (farmer's bridge), I drop to the side of the road intending to regroup, rest my sore toes, and change into my hiking sandals. But no sooner do I sit down, then up pulls a bright blue subcompact vehicle with a smiling, lone female driver inside, just like clockwork. And without further ado, *ma nouvelle amie francaise Ly* whisks me up, and we are buzzing along down the road *ensemble. Ly* has a small dog in the back seat in a carrier, and she explains in good English that she is helping a friend get the dog veterinary attention today. She also makes it her business to help pilgrims when she can since she lives in the area. The Camino must have rightly decided I need the help, bedraggled me. I don't protest. About two kilometers down the road, I am dropped off at a small, dirt, side road where the sign for *Coderc* points to the left, along with the familiar yellow and blue waymark. The Camino makes its turn here. *Merci beaucoup*,

Dear *Ly!* Oh, and just as *Ly* and I are searching for the Camino waymarks so as not to drive too far, out walks an elderly man into his yard, one *Ly* has decided is an Englishman based on his dapper, Cotswolds-looking attire. In real English, he also kindly points us to the left right by his home. Coincidence or serendipity?

For the next five miles, I walk "a path", several narrow "asphalt roads", and then "a long straight road past a water tower". I blame all this on Nancy Drew and the old mystery book series of the same name which I constantly had my nose in as a child. At the end, at the hamlet of Bouilloux, I take what becomes *Avenue Eugene Leroy* to a roundabout at *le Restaurant Saint Roch*, entering Thiviers. There is also a sign pointing left for my refuge for tonight, *Les Conches*. I intentionally opt for the steep, long climb straight ahead up *Rue du Général Lamy* into the *centre ville*. I stop for a *café au lait* and get directions to the nearest *Bureau de Poste* which, as it turns out, is relatively close by. I plan to mail certain things home *tout de suite*: my gold mirror and dish from Limoges; a battery charger I haven't used; my flipflops, ditto; gloves and hat, ditto; paperwork and maps I have used. They all drop like rocks into a mailing box at the post office. I waited in line and then fussed around for over an hour sorting through my rucksack and packing my box. In the meantime, a quick onslaught of rain has passed through just as this nice French woman is patiently helping me plug information into a machine for my box to go to the States.

I also pay a visit to the *Eglise Notre-Dame de l'Assumption* which is on one end of the tree-lined town square. This magnificent church, dating from the twelfth century, is of both Romanesque and Gothic architectural design. Its history is fascinating, having suffered ruin and rehabilitation over the centuries due to the religious wars, as well as influences of local power struggles and even the plague. Its looming bell tower, its vaulted ceiling in the cool, silvery stone nave, its paintings of Madonna and Child, its stone reliefs of Saint Michael, Joan of Arc, and Saint Roch, its brilliant stained-glass windows—must I leave it all so soon?

Now that the rain has stopped, I have turned on my GPS hoping to get to *Les Conches* a better way than retracing my steps back down the hill to the roundabout. Big mistake, for my GPS has sent me on another wild goose chase. I eventually do have to return from whence I have come back through the center of town and then down *Rue du Général Lamy* to the turnoff for my *gite. Les Conches* sits on a beautiful piece of farm property in the countryside overlooking Thiviers. *Madame Cordier* has been expecting me. I have a quaint, comfortable room and private bath in a cottage of two spaces. The moon is beginning to rise behind a backdrop of trees, and a chilly breeze echoes its own signal of approaching nightfall. I know, you thought I was exaggerating about getting to my refuge before dark.

Dinner at their "*le Bistrot*" consists of a cold veggie starter, a local pork dish with potatoes au gratin, *vin rouge* and baguettes, and a parfait for dessert. It is lovely and served at small tables in their cozy bar. I drag myself back over to my *gite* for bed, so glad to be here.

At *le petit déjeuner*, Mme. *Cordier* calls up her friend who has owned and run the *Hotel Les Aromes* in Négrondes for many years. I happened to say I wanted to stay there tonight since other villages on my map past Négrondes were too far away for a day's walk. I had gotten no response to my call or email. In speaking to her friend directly this morning, we see that Les Aromes is closed for now. *Madame* kindly agrees to transport me to the *gare* in Thiviers where I have now purchased a ticket for the large city of Périgueux. I have also called ahead to alert the *hospitalier* at *Refuge Pelerins* that I would be arriving.

Périgueux has been a major stop for pilgrims traveling the *Voie de Vézelay* since medieval times. Celtic and Gallic tribes settled here before the Roman conquest of the region. The

Isle River runs through Périgueux and probably provided commerce along its banks as well as fertile soil, for centuries. Even today, Périgueux is known for its *paté de foie gras* and for its *truffles*. Once at my destination, I follow other train passengers who have gotten off here down a broad, tree-lined street to a roundabout and then follow the signs left into the *centre ville* and the ancient part of town. I am headed to the *Cathédrale Saint-Front*, several kilometers away. Constructed in the tenth century, this Romanesque cathedral and its iconic bell tower and domes stand tall against the bright, French ultramarine blue sky. As I am adjusting my eyes to the interior dim light, I notice that a lovely, pale mint green permeates the area around the main altar in almost a soft fog. Equally stunning, huge circular brass chandeliers, decorated with clusters of white tapers, run down the arched ceiling of the nave. I sit for a while and take it all in. In a dark side chapel, a life-size, old, wooden statue of the pilgrim, Saint James, has, unmistakably, turned his head and peers directly at me as I approach him. He is surrounded with votive candles glowing red and gold, as well as missives of prayer requests laid at his feet and tucked in his arms. As I have on all my travels on the Camino, I wonder even now if he might walk with me as I, like so many, tread this ancient path. I am reluctant to leave.

But once outside, I manage to locate the *Office de Tourisme* at *11 Rue du Lys*. Friendly faces here have helped orient me to the city and have provided a map. The oh-so-delightful *Rue du Lys* itself is lined with colorful shops, and if you just look up, hot pink umbrellas dazzle overhead for a festive flair. A block away, people are congregated outside at tables underneath myriads of multi-colored balloons. It's pretty obvious they love their city and the simple, as well as sophisticated, pleasures it serves up. I have a picnic and café au lait on the town square and then retrace my steps back toward the *gare* and the Refuge de Pelerins on *83 Rue Gambetta*. Since pilgrims can't show up until after three o'clock, I have positioned myself for a rest inside another beautiful church just down the street from the *gite,* the *Eglise Saint-Martin*. A small, painted wooden pilgrim stands inside as well as a pristine, alabaster statue of *Sainte Thérese de Lisieux*. She holds a cascade of roses, and they surround her at her feet. Theresa, the little flower, is venerated around the world. Drawn to a contemplative life like her two sisters, she entered the Carmelite Convent of Lisieux, in Normandy, but then succumbed to tuberculosis when she was just twenty-five years old. Her devotion, it seems, and her life were complete.

Rap, rap, rap…it is just past three o'clock, and I want to settle in at the *gite* for the night. I hear some muted activity and then the sound of someone bounding down the stairs. The door flings open to the smiling, almost mischievous face of the *hospitalier*. *Bonjour, Madame; je suis Johnna, la pelerine Americaine*, I offer. *Ah oui, entrez! Karine* excitedly ushers me into a main hallway with a dark room to the left. She instructs me to place all the things I want to take upstairs in a plastic bin that is provided and to leave my boots on a rack next to my backpack. She is busy; other pilgrims are arriving, and she is also reviewing passports and stamping pilgrim credentials, checking people in upstairs. So helpful, this one. After the dust settles, Karine and I sit together and review my possible next stops on the Camino and the *gites* she recommends. Karine has also walked the *Voie de Vézela*, and she has decided opinions about my itinerary moving forward, including her suggestion that I take the train on some of the upcoming portions, just as she did. It is so noted.

I have been assigned to one of the three small dormitory rooms. I have chosen a bed by the far window in one corner of the room. One other female pilgrim arrives and occupies the bed just across from mine. There is one other bed in our room, and it is empty. The Vézelay Route is generally less traveled than the other routes through France, so I have fortunately been able to obtain a bed easily, that is, if the *gite* is open. For twenty euros, I have a clean, comfortable little bed and *le petit déjeuner*. Who could complain about that? For dinner, I am having pasta in a cup of boiling water alongside two or three other pilgrims seated at the kitchen table. We share our Camino stories as best we can, in our multiple languages. Our smiles require no translation.

I am delighted to reconnect at breakfast with the pilgrim couple I had met at the *gite* in La Coquille. They arrived last night after I did. Unfortunately, he has fallen, hurt his back, and has broken a rib. Disappointed, they are headed home today on the train to northern France. Sometimes simply taking a rest for a few days helps sore feet and muscles, but not here, not this time. I am reminded of when I first walked the Camino on the Frances Route in Spain in 1998. Leaving the monastery at Samos, I badly twisted my ankle and tore ligaments. I ended up walking to Santiago on crutches with a black and blue swollen leg and ankle and the assistance of pain pills. I was fortunate, but this experience with *mes amis francais* is different. The Camino offers solace and protection; it also sometimes serves up harsh reality, like life in general,

According to Karine, I go left out of the *gite* and then turn right and head straight out of Périgueux. I am headed for Saint-Astier which is almost fifteen miles away. I have reserved a room and *le petit déjeuner* for thirty euros, the pilgrim rate, at a new *chambre d'hote* with *Madame Genevieve,* also at Karine's suggestion. I reach the now familiar roundabout leaving town, by the *gare*. I walk a pleasant road past more roundabouts, then by a cycle path, and under a railway bridge. At the *Abbaye de Chancelade,* I turn left up a very steep, wooded path to a pinpoint of light at the top. Next come narrow asphalt roads and twists and turns until I finally reach the hamlet of Terrassononie. Past the hamlet, I am ascending again, now through a dense forest. Holy solitude, perhaps. Loneliness, no.

I am also being careful and trying not to tempt fate. I have picked up a suitable *baton de randonnée* in the woods. It has quietly volunteered its help, if I agree to return it to nature after its mission is complete. My new hiking pole helps me feel more secure, as isolated as it is out here.

For lunch I am having leftover slices of baguettes and butter that I have saved from breakfast, as well as fresh figs from overhanging fig trees and even grapes from wild vines along the side of the road. By now, I am walking a steep descent and then through hamlets and the villages of Gravelle and Annesse. My walk eventually takes me on an asphalt bike path for miles between fields of parched corn fields. The corn looks black, as if it never got a chance to be harvested, it is so dry here. And as I look up, clouds have formed in dense waves, but there is still no rain. For myself, I am glad for that, but not for the land. Wildfires came to southwestern France this year with alarming results. I cross the Isle River via a bicycle bridge and weave my way around a canal. Near another bridge approaching Saint-Astier, I turn left and learn only later, I went the wrong direction. It doesn't pay to be too smug and miss the signals in life. Several kilometers later, I find myself in the outer reaches of the village of *Lidl at* a large Carrefour. People look at me like I just emerged from Alice's Wonderland with the Mad Hatter. I must look frightful. But now, I have been able to reach my host *Mme. Genevieve* on my cellphone as I am sitting outside on a bench. *Genevieve* had given up on me, thinking I was just another fickle pilgrim who had changed plans but never let her know. After all, it *is* almost six o'clock. I am profusely grateful she is coming for me.

Mme Genevieve has shown me to a comfortable room with a bath upstairs in her home. After a shower, I walk over to a *supermarché* several blocks away to buy something for dinner. I eat with *Genevieve* at the bar in her kitchen, and we share some red wine I had bought and lugged home. I bet I have walked eighteen miles today, not that I am complaining. But can I go to bed now? Yes, you can *Madame*. Sweet dreams!

After *le petit déjeuner*, I walk into the *centre ville* of Saint-Astier which is only a few blocks away. A play is being performed here complete with local actors in medieval costumes. Unfortunately, the church is closed, so I walk back by a carousel and by *la*

Mairie, the town hall, with its cascade of hot-pink flowers. This is another charming village in the Dordogne. It also has a *gare,* and after some tortured French-English conversation with *Mme. Genevieve,* she insists on walking with me to the train station nearby for my rail passage to Mussidan. She doesn't want me to get lost again, I suspect. Not on her watch.

Mussidan is a mid-sized town about fifteen miles away. I am hoping to check in at the *Office de Tourisme* to secure a bed at the *Refuge Municipal.* But by the time I have walked several miles from the train station into the *centre ville* and then to the tourist office, it has closed. Today is Saturday, and it closed at noon. It is almost four o'clock, and I have no place to stay. Since I know the church is always central to the community, I walk over to the one nearby, at *Rue Saint-Agnan.* The Vézelay Route also picks up here according to my pilgrim walking guide. The *Eglise Saint-George* is another beautiful, old church on the Camino. It is open, and I rest in its cool nave for a while wondering what to do next. Now, in consulting my list of accommodations as I sit outside on a step, I call up *Madame Simon* who has a *chambre d'hote.* She rather miraculously answers, but the real miracle is that her *gite* is just across the street from the church. She quickly walks over, rather than try to explain her location, and before I barely realize my good fortune, I have a lovely private room and a kitchenette reserved just for pilgrims.

Bruno, a Frenchman, arrived after me last night, and this morning we are sharing *le petit déjeuner,* the usual suspects—yogurt, baguettes and butter and jam, croissants, café au lait that *Mme. Simon* laid out for us. Bruno tried to get into the *Refuge Municipal* as I had initially hoped to do, but was turned away because he arrived late, shortly after their four o'clock deadline. Fortunately, he also came upon Mme. Simon's *chambre d'hote* late in the day by happy coincidence. He is out first, but it's not the last time I will run into him. Last night, *Mme. Simon* called the *gite* at the hamlet of La Gratade, nine miles away, and left a message on my behalf with *Madame Villaud*. We got no response, but I am hopeful there will be room for me there; twenty euros for a bed and *le petit déjeuner*.

In consulting my walking guide, with my back to the church, I turn left to leave Mussidan. Ascending, I am directed up several asphalt roads, then to an unpaved road, then to a dirt path, then to a "forest road" which goes on forever, it seems. At this point, I don't know if I would feel better meeting up with another human being or not. Either way presents its fears and challenges in this isolation. The soft leaf-strewn wisdom path of the woods should be a comfort to me. After all, it serves as a walking meditation. I am attempting to be quiet and hear its whisper, but, instead, I find myself chattering out loud about many things. Today, it is my sorrow over losing my little cat Grayson. I walk on, my new hiking pole having to hear it all.

As the old saying goes, "I wander, but I am not lost". To add a little levity here, Bruno *does* get lost. He took a left after we shared some *biscuits* together sitting on the side of the road. Only after he had walked on did I notice that the Vézelay Route continued straight ahead through the hamlet. He told me, miles later, that he had walked an alternate much longer loop, much to his dismay.

I have crossed under a highway and over a small bridge, as per my guide. I also walked through the hamlet of Les Jaunies. Past the wider asphalt road of the D-20, I eventually reach the stately old church at the hamlet of Saint-Géry. The church bells begin to toll upon my arrival, as if beckoning *me* inside. This has happened more than once; I have noticed but tried to explain away the synchronicity. Now, I embrace it with a smile. I am reminded of divine timing and the order in seeming chaos. A statue of *Saint-Géry* awaits me inside. He stands as a monument to those children who died in the two world wars. This church must have comforted many parishioners over these many years. Their prayers are palatable; it also now comforts me. As if this wasn't enough, a beautiful statue of *Sainte-Jeanne d'Arc*, wielding her sword, is mounted on the wall across from *St-Gery*. She is dressed in her characteristic silver coat of arms and a light blue, flowing, long skirt. She proudly holds a white flag embellished with gold *fleurs-de-lis*. I painted her years ago. Joan of Arc has always been a symbol of strength and fortitude for me and just what I need at this moment. About three more miles and I turn a sharp right off a narrow asphalt road in the forest and then take another turn to La Gratade. At the top of the hill, I locate *Madame Villaud's* home and the attached *gite.* Apparently, *Mme. Villaud* is not here yet from work, but her small *gite is* open. And the French pilgrim that I had roomed with at the *gite* in Périgueux i*s* here. We greet each other with mutual excitement in seeing familiar, friendly pilgrim faces. I take the lower bunk across from hers. There are spaces for five pilgrims, but just the two of us tonight. Her married French friends are parked on the property in their camper; tomorrow they all leave the Camino to head back to their homes. We share cups of instant pasta and baguettes for an early supper. Our hand laundry is drying out in the late afternoon sun, and as the chill at dusk begins to set in, I hurry out to retrieve it. Sleep comes my way easily tonight.

This morning, I have my sights set on the *Chateau Puy Servain* and its *gite d'etape,* ten miles away. According to my list of pilgrim accommodations, it offers a dormitory with six spaces and an evening meal with wine from the domain. It is a bright, beautiful day, just right for a hike. I walk through two small villages, Fraisse and Monfaucon, and then begin a descent, crossing a small bridge. But what goes down also goes up, and I find myself walking steep asphalt, narrow roads through two hamlets and then a long forest footpath under the shade of the trees. I also now cross through fields stretched out under the blazing sun and then continue up by a huge winery and its surrounding vineyards. The heat of the day has caught up with me. I stop, changing into my hiking sandals, because walking these steep hills has pushed my toes into the end of my boots. Ouch! At the top of the hill, overlooking the vineyards, a sign reads "A journey of a thousand miles begins with one step." by Paulo Coelho, the Brazilian novelist. He would know since he, too, had walked the Camino and then wrote an enchanting tale about it. But my favorite book of his is, by far, *The Alchemist*, another fantastical tale of the hero who leaves home to seek his fortune, only to return eventually, after many struggles, with the simple wisdom that the true happiness he sought was seeking him, at home.

After the hamlet of Cap de Fer, I walk along another, long, forested road to its end and then turn right and then another immediate right toward the *Chateau Puy Servain*. At the end of this road, a half mile up, no one is around at what appears to be the offices for the chateau. But a sign for the *gite* points to a huge open barn where farming equipment is kept. And up a long flight of stone steps in the barn, I discover a large rustic sitting area and open kitchen. Up another flight of stairs, I find the dormitory room and claim my little bed on the opposite wall by a window. Only one other bed is taken which I learn later is that of a young French woman who is doing an internship at the winery. She speaks English well and tells me she is working on the early stages of a degree in viticulture, hopefully, to become a *sommelier*, a wine maker, some day. We don't have long to wait before the door flings open, and three more pilgrims arrive. Boisterous are these guys, friendly, and fun. They are *mes nouveaux amis de pelerins de Hollande*. All of them Dutch engineers, they are walking this segment of their yearly journey on the Vézelay Route. Not yet retired, they hope someday to reach Santiago de Compostela in segments. *Madame Hecquet* arrives next and delivers our meals, which must be heated, as well as bottles of red wine from the winery. She also leaves us with fresh *baguettes* for our dinner as well as for *le petit déjeuner*. After *le diner*, the guys clear the table and wash the dishes, despite their light-hearted jabs and winks that this is women's work best left to me, but they don't want my help. And as they start their nightcaps in the sitting area, I am already happily tucked in my bed upstairs, the windows closed to keep out the mosquitos, as well as the cool night air. I don't wake up when they come up to bed, although I do awake to an occasional snore, or as my French pilgrim women friends call it, a "snork".

Today I am heading to Sainte-Foy-la-Grande, only five miles from here. My fellow pilgrims huddled outside the *gite* in the foggy morning light long enough for me to take their photo, and then they were off without me. We all know that they walk at a faster pace. Amazingly, I also now prefer my solitude. At the end of the road, I regained the Camino and turn right. About a mile up, I am directed left onto a grassy footpath across fields toward the ruins of an old mill, *La Rouquette,* standing at the top of a hill. I climb this hill and turn left by the mill according to the Camino waymarks. Then, I go down a small trail through very dense woods, only to emerge at the other end within sight of the road to the *gite,* from last night. I essentially, unwittingly, doubled back to where I started this morning. *Alors*, so being lost, I hastily retrace my steps back through the woods and up to the mill again. And then I see that I had missed the correct turn left and should have gone slightly farther, past a hedge, and then turned left. Diddling and dawdling this morning, that's me, but at least I am back on track.

I carry on at the edge of vineyards and then turn right on a wider dirt road into the forest, onto what looks like a bike path for those on the Camino *a vélo.* In fact, two cyclists have already passed me by. I weave through the hamlet of Brait until, eventually, I am directed onto a "steep and dangerous descent" on a narrow path through woods, the path from hell. Sharp, jagged rocks and a slippery dirt trail straight down are the order of the day. And don't worry about stepping on a *serpent*, even snakes won't tread this path if they don't have to. This goes on for over a mile. When I emerge out of the woods, I collapse on an old bench by the leafy, dark, forest hole I just climbed out of. The bench overlooks vineyards, a vast valley, and the city of Port-Sainte-Foy off in the distance. But there is no clear Camino way marker as to where I exactly go from here; I am not a crow, at

Walking West on the Camino—on the Vézelay Route   101

least not yet. After more dawdling, I follow the vineyards down the hill, cross the D20, and then at the *Dordogne* River, I turn right by a bridge and reach the church and the pilgrim hostel across the street. Both are closed until much later in the day. By now, I have changed into my hiking sandals because my sore toes complained so badly. Two young teens, standing outside smoking cigarettes and looking at me perplexed, after some amount of conversation between us in French, point me in the direction of the long bridge over the Dordogne where I cross and reach the outskirts of the sister city of Sainte-Foy-la-Grande.

I follow the signs into the *centre ville* and to the *Office de Tourisme*; at least they might have recommendations for where I might stay tonight. The tourist office is closed too, but a nice young man, working by an open window inside, kindly directs me over to the *Hotel-Restaurant de la Gare,* at the other end of town, just across from the train station. The *Hotel de la Gare* was the only accommodation on my list for Sainte-Foy-la-Grande, but I had overlooked it.

Ste. Foy-la-Grande is an especially beautiful city. Most notably, the Camino takes me by the *Eglise-de-Sainte-Foy-la-Grande.* This church, dedicated to Saint Foy, has its own fascinating history. It is believed that Benedictine monks from the great Abbey at Conques constructed a church as early as 812 A.D. near the Dordogne, which then became a place of pilgrimage and stopping off point on the Way of Saint James. In the thirteenth century, the Knights Templars built on the current site, although parts of the church were later destroyed during the Wars of Religion. In 1622, Louis XIII ordered the ruins be restored. Donations from King Louis the XIV completed the work. By 1876, the Pope proclaimed Saint Foy to be the patron saint of the city and sent a purported relic of the saint from the Abbey. Born in *Agen* in central France, Foy was beheaded in 303 for her Christian faith, at the age of thirteen. *Foy*, from the old French, meaning faith. I am familiar with Saint Foy having stayed at the Abbey in Conques on a previous pilgrimage on the Le Puy Route. A stunning, golden reliquary of her is displayed at the abbey museum.

The ancient church of Saint-Foy-le-Grande proudly bears the familiar placard at its door which signals its importance on the Route, as a major *halte*. It is the "Chemin de Compostelle" in blue, embellished with two gold scallop shells. Inside the church, life-size iron cutouts of early pilgrims, shells hanging from their necks, seem to stride across the back of the nave. They are holding their staffs and their gourds in a firm resolve. Two lovely stained-glass windows of Saint Foy shimmer in the invading sunlight, and a colorful statue of Saint James frames one side of the altar. I sit for a while and soak up the majesty of this holy place, holy because of the prayers said here, most likely, for centuries. And then I go on. I am intent on finding a bed for the night. In starts and stops, I have reached the *Hotel de la Gare*. I can secure a room here and *le petit déjeuner* at the pilgrim rate. The restaurant was closed until eight o'clock for dinner. By then, I will be sound asleep. I get directions and walk over to a Carrefour several blocks away to pick up something for dinner: yogurt, mixed nuts, cheese. What should have been a five-mile hike today has turned into one of at least ten miles. But I am not really complaining. I love this little family-run hotel and my cozy room. And tomorrow, I am taking the train to Mont-de-Marsan. I have already bought my ticket.

The city of Mont-de-Marsan is another major stop on the Camino, not only now, but also during the Middle Ages. The capital of the *Landes*, in *Nouvelle-Aquitaine*, Mont-de-Marsan sits at the convergence of two rivers which, together, become the *Midouze*. It is little wonder a vibrant community emerged here to assist pilgrims along the Way of Saint James. What also developed was a deep reverence for Mary Magdalene.

Once in Mont-de-Marsan, using my familiar game plan, I follow the signs leading from the railway station to the *centre ville* and to the Office de Tourisme. The tourist office, once a tenth-century windmill, sits on the picturesque banks of the

Midouze River. A small metal sculpture of a diver is beautifully and delicately suspended over the river here, highlighting the importance of sculpture for the city, as well as for its sports arenas. Using a map, I walk to the left out of the tourist office past *Place Charles de Gaulle* and then to the right toward *Rue Victor Hugo*, heading for the *Eglise de la Madeleine*. But first, I stop to enjoy *une pizza du terroir, La Francaise*, outside at *La Madeleine*, a delightful *brasserie* and *café*, painted in a pretty French yellow and blue, located near the church. Being both the pilgrim and the tourist, I have already sent pictures home to my sister.

The Church of the Madeleine stands shimmering under the rays of the afternoon sun. It sits on the Vézelay Route which passes squarely through the city. There is precious little information about this magnificent church. Like Mary herself, it seems to be an enigma. Around 1825, the church was built on the ruins of an old, Gothic, fourteenth-century parish church, dedicated to Mary Magdalene, which had collapsed. Even earlier, Mary Magdalene had been chosen the patroness saint of Mont-de-Marsan when the city was founded, in the twelfth century. Her influence must have been immense. The architect Arthaud is credited with rebuilding the church in its current Neoclassical, Greco-Roman design, with its four Doric columns and its triangular, ornamental pediment crowning the porch. As their bells toll, two square towers reach for the bright blue sky. I simply stand in front of the church in awe, transported back in time to its early splendor. A lovely statue of Mary Magdalene, holding a large urn or vase, greets those who enter her temple. She is smiling and perhaps for good reason.

I am even more awed by the interior. Its vaulted ceiling is designed with circular motifs of cherubs among white clouds, with blue and pink. The whole nave glows lavender and green in the soft, dazzling light. A high white altar stands at the front of the nave underneath two huge, crystal chandeliers. Panoramic, colorful frescoes of the life of the Magdalen are positioned on the wall above the altar. There is the wedding at Cana; there is another scene, presumably of Mary Magdalene, draped in gold and white, wiping Jesus's feet with her long, auburn hair; there is a scene just after the crucifixion where Jesus is surrounded by two women and one other, along with Mary Magdalene; there is Jesus standing outside in his burial cloth. Mary Magdalene is kneeling in front of him with the alabaster jar. One *Madame Grimaud-Baudit*, her husband, and an Italian gilder are credited with painting the frescoes. I can find no other information on *Madame* or her frescoes. It seems that *Madame Grimaud-Baudit* is herself a mystery, as well as her rather curious, evocative paintings. Art historians may have answers. More likely, the true significance of the frescoes, like Saint Mary Magdalene, will remain lost in time and just beyond our reach.

But what might be even more interesting are the stained-glass windows. In one, Mary Magdalene stands in a boat, in red, white, and purple robes. Her arms are outstretched, the waves tossing and turning at her feet. There are others huddled beneath her, a young woman, as well as perhaps the Blessed Mary, the mother of Jesus, dressed in blue. There is another stained-glass masterpiece with Mary Magdalene kneeling before Jesus in the garden. Jesus holds a long spade or gardening tool. Unmistakably, winding at their feet is a vine, an esoteric symbol for the Davidic bloodline. Both are crowned in glimmering halos of light. Another is one of the Magdalen kneeling before an open book and a skull in a cave, in reference to her time purportedly spent in southern France as a mystic. Aside from the stained glass, there is also a rather astounding, eighteenth-century painting showing Jesus laid out in burial clothes beneath the cross, with most likely the Blessed Mary, John, as well as a few others standing nearby. Mary Magdalene, depicted in her now-familiar robes of red and white, leans over him, inconsolable.

Mary Magdalene has been elevated here from her tired, worn-out, perhaps erroneous place in history as the penitent prostitute. What did they know, these painters and artisans, and sculptors? I am reminded that Pope Gregory, in a series of speeches about the Magdalen in 591 A.D., and within the context of the great plague in Europe, as well as efforts to promote clerical chastity, openly accused Mary of improper behavior. Yet, there is nothing in the Bible that suggests this. "It is clear, *brothers*, he said…" It was not until 1969 that the Roman Catholic Church apologized for that misrepresentation of her. Her feast day is July 22 when she is celebrated, especially here in Mont-de-Marsan, where they hold festivals in her honor and parade her image down the street.

I am on my way back across the river to the *Refuge Pelerins* which is run by the *Amis de Saint Jacques*, at *2 Rue Augustin Lesbazeille*. As suggested by my list of accommodations, I have called and registered ahead of time. For a donation, I have a little bed in a dormitory room with two or three other pilgrims. The *hospitalier* shows up later to check us in and stamp our pilgrim passports. There are no meals here, but I am happy to eat my leftover pizza from lunch. Even though I arrived in Mont-de-Marsan by train this morning, I have walked far and wide through the city today. It is time for bed.

The last of my cold pizza for breakfast, and I am off. I can hardly call it a *petit déjeuner*. I am trying to get ahead of the Dutch couple who were with me at the *gite* last night. She is walking; he follows along on his bike or detours for their groceries. Just for once, I would like to walk with or near someone else. I figure she will catch up with me. However, I missed the left turn onto Rue Gambetta and had to double back when I finally figured it out. And sure enough, here is my fellow pilgrim, Carla, heading correctly down Rue Gambetta just in front of me. I am now racing along at her pace so that I can, at least, keep her in my sights. Lucky for her, because she heads to the left incorrectly as we leave the outer reaches of the city. I call out to her to follow me to the right—imagine that. Serendipity has its way with us, or is it karmic help, or both. She had also helped me earlier to negotiate some confusing roundabouts. The road eventually turns into a gravel road and then an unpaved road "through a pine forest." Carla has long since passed me by. But forests and solitude have become my friends now, sort of. It stretches on for what seems like miles and miles.

More than five miles later, I have reached the village of Benguet and its church. As has happened more than once, the bells at the *Eglise Saint Jean Baptist* begin to toll as I approach. How can I not pay this lovely, old church a visit? Reconstructed after it fell into ruin in the sixteenth century, it was ceremoniously reopened at Easter in 1888. Its stained-glass windows sparkle in the light of the afternoon sun. A stone bas-relief of The Last Supper is displayed in the nave. Interestingly too, a Templar *croix rouge*, or red cross, has been carved into every pillar, for those with eyes to see.

It is hot. I am relieved to find another church a few miles up, the primitive, old church of Saint-Christau. Its doors stand wide open as if to beckon pilgrims inside to shelter them from the heat. A rope used to ring the bells hangs from the belfry in the middle of the doorsill. After a brief rest, I go on. I want to stop for the night at Saint-Sever, thirteen miles for today. I have reserved a room at *Hotel des Arceaux*, a small family-owned hotel and restaurant on my list. If I arrive there between four and six o'clock when it is closed, I will need to call, and someone will come over and check me in.

I am out of water. At the little hamlet of Sainte Eulalie, I am directed by my guidebook to turn right by the church and go down a narrow asphalt path by a dike and then along the Adour River. I have looked for water, but the church doesn't seem to be open, and the elementary school is locked. I make that right, but then I must simply sit down. Desperation knocking, I leave my pack by the side of the path and walk back to the turn at the school. By now, a young woman has driven up, probably to pick up her child. After my question in rough French as to whether she has any water, she, smiling with sudden recognition, hands me a large bottle of cold water that she happens to have in the front seat of her car. *Merci beaucoup, Madame,* I manage to say. Before I doubled back, I got to experience myself in another rather unflattering meltdown, like the wicked witch in Dorothy's OZ. *Does the Camino really provide? What am I going to do?* And so, it went. Now, greatly refreshed, I pick up my backpack again and walk on. About a hundred feet farther along, I look down to see a five-euro bill just sitting here on the path, as if it were waiting just for me. So yes, the Camino *does* provide, in strange and wonderful ways. It is also not very smart to run out of water; I won't do it again.

I had thought I was much closer to Saint-Sever by now. Not so. The path by the Adour is lovely, but long. And at one point, I must go back for my sunglasses that I had dropped on a bench. I eventually turn left on a long bridge over the Adour for the entrance into the ancient city of *Saint-Sever*. My guidebook directs me to "ascend to the city", and go up I do on a steep, broad thoroughfare above the river valley and the vineyards and hills of the Chalosse. My backpack must rest some at benches strategically placed up the hill. There is much renovation in town, but I get directions from construction workers to the *centre ville* and the *Office de Tourisme*. It is obvious the tourist office caters to pilgrims and to those tourists interested in the Camino. Large, colorful placards with photos and art on the historic sites of the Vézelay Route abound. A staff member provides me with a map and history of *St.-Sever* in English and kindly points me across the square to the cathedral. She recommends my lodging tonight at *Hotel des Arceaux* which I had already booked. She also suggests I stay a second night, this time at the old *Couvent et Cloitre des Jacobins*, a UNESCO World Heritage site, now a municipal refuge for pilgrims. The tourist office holds the password to the *gite*, so I show my pilgrim credentials and sign up for tomorrow night. I am glad to stay two nights in this lovely, medieval *ville* that has helped pilgrims for centuries. It is also supposed to rain tomorrow, so this is a perfect opportunity for a day's rest.

The old *Abbaye de Saint-Sever,* just across from the tourist office, is still open, so I walk over for a visit before I check in at the *Hotel des Arceaux*. The Benedictine, Romanesque abbey church was founded in the late tenth century by *Guillaume Sanche,* Count of *Gascony,* after he defeated the invading Vikings. In 1060, after a fire, the monks rebuilt in the model of the great monastery at Cluny. In the sixteenth century, the abbey suffered damage again and was reconstructed after the 100 Years War between the Catholics and the Protestants. It is distinguished by its seven apses, the one most striking, a semi-circular dome or vault high above the main altar. Gold chandeliers, glistening in the dim light, line both sides of the nave. The capitals and columns are also stunning, colorfully painted orange and green and gold. They date from the Gallo-Roman period. Magnificent paintings decorate the walls, one of the Blessed Mary trampling the serpent, as well as another of the baptism of Jesus by John the Baptist. A beautiful alabaster statue of Joan of Arc greets those who enter. But this ancient nave has a further story to tell.

According to medieval legend, Saint Severus was commissioned by the Pope to evangelize the region of Gascony in the early fifth century. At some point, Severus warned the Roman governor, Adrian, of the approach of the Vandals. In revenge, Severus was decapitated by these barbarians, and he was said to have climbed the steep hill there carrying his head. His relics are purportedly interned at the abbey in a large, gold reliquary which I notice in a side chamber. This abbey church gained much prominence and power in the region during the Middle Ages. One might see why.

The *Hotel et Le Bistrot des Arceaux* is located close by the town square. I have a small room and private bathroom just off the interior courtyard. After an early supper at a small table in the bar area, I am tucked in my bed and content. The French word *contente* means happy, and that might be an even better description of my mood tonight, glad to have walked the Camino today, and most happy to be at my *halte.* It was a long day. I understand now how Severus must have felt carrying his head up that hill, I carried mine too.

After a lovely *petit déjeuner,* I settle my bill and spend some time walking the narrow, cobblestoned streets of Saint-Sever. I have also located a small market where I have purchased supplies for dinner tonight as well as for my hike tomorrow morning. The tourist office called the *hospitalier* at the *gite* who allowed me to check in early, by noon. This is good since it is drizzling rain now, and I have huddled at the tourist office for as long as I am permitted before they close for lunch and before I make a complete nuisance of myself. Age has its perks sometimes, as does the look of a drowned rat.

The Cloitre et Couvent des Jacobins was established as a Dominican convent in the thirteenth century. The Dominicans were both a contemplative and a preaching order of nuns and monks. Saint Dominic, a Spanish monk, is known for his efforts to convert the heretical sect of the gnostic Cathars in the Languedoc to orthodox Catholicism, but to do it peacefully. He was met with little success. Finally, the inquisitionists prevailed. In 1244, the Albigensian Crusade culminated with hundreds of Cathars being burned at the stake at Montsegur. Men, women, and children went to their deaths willingly rather than convert. The history of southern France is complicated and intense.

The *gite* at the Convent of the Jacobins has twelve beds. For thirteen euros, I am in a cozy upstairs bedroom painted green. My lower bunkbed is situated by a beautiful, old, round window that opens inward with a view of the street below. There is no one else here tonight except for Kristen, a Belgian pilgrim. She takes a lower bunk across from mine. Kristen has already walked to Santiago de Compostela from Saint-Jean-Pied-de-Port, but she wants to walk the Vézelay Route to complete her Camino. We share pasta for dinner and stories of our lives. It has grown cold and rather windy, and we have closed the shutters for more insulation and warmth before we turn in.

Kristen is a little powerhouse of energy, faster than me. She retraced her steps a couple of blocks to buy some croissants at a *patisserie* and walked on. Also up early, I ate *quelques tranches de pain et beurre* and had instant coffee. We must walk as far as we can before the rain starts. My walking goal today is Hagetmau, a sizeable French *ville* in the Basque Region. It is over ten miles away. I hope to stay at the *Refuge Municipal* at *434 Rue Saint Girons*. Reservations cannot be made. You show your pilgrim credentials and pay 8,40 euros at the city recreational and pool site and then receive the password for entry to the *gite.* There are no meals.

From the *Cloitre des Jacobins*, my walking guide directs me straight ahead down *Rue du Général Lamarque*, then down *Rue de la Guillerie* to leave Saint-Sever. After a while, with more twists and turns in the outskirts of town and then into a rural area, I turn left at a large sports stadium, finally turn a sharp left again onto a gravel road by a water tower. The clouds have turned an ominous gray, and I can hear the crackle of thunder and lightning in the distance. I pick up my pace. I cross the bridge at the *Gabas* stream, follow a small asphalt road along the railroad and pass a stone railroad bridge. I eventually reach the small village of Audignon, but not before a torrent of cold rain begins to fall from a dark, tumultuous sky. I am at least grateful that there is no lightning directly overhead, although water is now dripping off my nose and pooling into my boots, despite my jacket and rain cape. The few pages of my walking guide for today's hike are wet, the ink blurred, never mind my best efforts to keep them dry. Audignon is deserted. I follow the traditional yellow and blue waymarks of the Camino posted on trees and buildings which help me, although they are few and far between. This should suffice, surely.

I have walked along more paths by the railroad, ascending and descending to the hamlet of Horsarrieu "on the other side of the valley", as my hapless, soggy written directions have indicated. Finally, entering Hagetmau, I disregard the signs to the right for the *Crypte de Saint-Girons* and walk straight ahead toward the *centre ville*. I am soon met by a friendly man standing on the road who is a fellow pilgrim and is staying several kilometers past Hagetmau. He has walked back into town for the day, he says. I am a bit curious. Why would anyone walk back on the Camino? Each step matters on a long journey like this and must be calculated. I keep straight into town, turning left by a stone fountain and then left again several more blocks up by a *magasin de chaussures*, (shoe store). The rain had slacked off, but now it picks up again as I wander along looking for the municipal pool where I can reserve a bed for the night at the *gite*.

Mission finally accomplished, I retrace my steps back to the stone fountain and then take the turn toward the Crypt of St. Girons, heading across town in the other direction. I meet up with the same man who just seems to be loitering near the *gite*. He encourages me to go see the crypt which is just a little farther down the road from the *Refuge Municipal*. "Okay, thanks", I say, and I wait until he rounds the bend. Once I locate the municipal pilgrim *gite*, I let myself in with the password. I had already discarded my hiking pole in the bushes by the *gite*; it broke entirely into two pieces due to the rain. Upstairs in the cold, stone dormitory room, I take off my backpack and muddy shoes and look around. Not more than two minutes later, I am hastily back out the door. If other pilgrims were staying here, I would feel better. But not tonight. The woman at the pool who checked me in told me that no one else had reserved, but me. Trust is one thing; right discernment is quite another. I am spooked by that man I have run into twice on the street. Perhaps he poses no danger at all. But better to listen to my inner voice and move on. Besides, I know I won't get one minute of sleep if I stay here tonight. I write this mostly for those fellow female pilgrims who walk or want to walk the Camino *seule*. Be not afraid but be vigilant and pay attention to your intuition.

The sun, hidden behind the clouds in the dusky, early evening sky, sits low on the pink horizon. It is a signal to seek shelter for the night, but where do I go now? I retrace my steps to a café and inquire about a room from a young waitress whom I had met earlier. Each piece seems to fit into a puzzle. She points me toward an inn in the lovely, old part of town not too far away. Once there, I am told they are full, but before I can barely turn around to leave, the innkeeper sends me out the door with her mother. This woman, who struggles to understand my version of French, drives me, first, by a house where an English woman runs out to explain what was going on. Next, I am whisked over to the *Hotel-Restaurant La Cremaillere* on the very edge leaving town along the Camino, the sweetest, most accommodating, family-owned hotel anyone might wish for. The innkeeper had made it her business to call ahead and make sure I would have a room. It must be an unspoken rule among the innkeepers and *hospitaliers* along the Camino to *work* tirelessly to accommodate us pilgrims if they possibly can. You have my heartfelt gratitude. *Merci beaucoup, a vous tous!*

Within minutes, I am unpacking in a lovely little room at *La Cremaillere*, booked in at the pilgrim rate, complete with *le diner et le petit déjeuner* in their restaurant. I highly recommend *La Cremaillere's* cheeseburger, *des pommes frites, et une salade verte*. Also, their *glace coco*. And did I mention their *vin rouge maison?* I have already sent a photo of this splendid array of culinary delights to my sister. She makes me check in with her every night, and tonight she's jealous. Rightly so. My, how fortunes can change just around the corner. *Bon appetit!*

It is Sunday, and *Monsieur* has closed the hotel-restaurant so that he can spend the day with his son. He has arranged with *Madame Nathalie* in Sault-de-Navailles to swing by the hotel and pick me up at one o'clock on her way home from her nursing job in Hagetmau. I had literally limped into the hotel last night with a sore, swollen left ankle. Since Nathalie was the only one recommended on my list of pilgrim accommodations, I had called her and left a message to arrange a room at her *chambre d'hote* for tonight. But *Monsieur* and *Nathalie* decided among themselves that I was in no shape to walk the thirteen kilometers, eleven miles, this morning to Sault-de-Navailles and arranged to commandeer my journey today. I must have looked frightful. Check-out time at the hotel is ten a.m., but I am parked on a chair in the hotel's small foyer enjoying *café au lait*, a pear, and cheese, courtesy of *Monsieur*, with instructions to lock the hotel's front door behind me when I leave. I will never forget their kindness shown to me, ever.

Sault-de-Navailles is a *petite* village in the *Pyrénées-Atlantiques* department, in the *Nouvelle Aquitaine* region of southwestern France. *Nathalie* and her husband are gracious hosts serving those few pilgrims who walk the Vézelay Route. She rents out an upstairs bedroom and shares meals with us at her family's table. Tonight, her husband has prepared a tasty chicken dish with pasta and vegetables, as well as his specialty dessert crepes. *Ma nouvelle amie pelerine*, Kristen, who shared the *gite* with me in *Saint-Sever*, had occupied my room last night. That speedy girl is one day ahead of me now. Soon enough, I sink into my warm covers, my ankle on the mend, and fall into a deep sleep.

This morning, after *croissants, toasted baguettes*, and *café au lait*, Nathalie insists on driving me past the church to the outskirts of Sault-de-Navailles to a more industrial, busy area where the Camino heads in the direction of Orthez, ten miles hence. I managed to call ahead and leave a message with the *hospitalier* at *Refuge Pelerins Hotel de la Lune*, run by the *Amis de Saint Jacques*, that I hoped to stay there tonight. Again, as is the custom with most municipal pilgrim gites, no reservations can be made. On the *Voie de Vézelay*, beds in gites seem easier to obtain than on the much more crowded *Frances Route* through northern Spain. Many of those pilgrims are out when it's still dark, donning their headlights, to secure a bed early, especially closer to Santiago de Compostela. Not so on the Vézelay Route, although some of the *gites* have closed due to the pandemic.

Packed up with leftover dessert crepes, a croissant, and water, I am dropped off at the other end of a small parking area with instructions to walk straight ahead on an unpaved road. The familiar waymarks of the Camino have come into view, my "home sweet home".

At the end of this road, I turn left ascending on a narrow, steep path through woods for miles and miles. I continue "along the slope of a hill" and then "cross a small forest." What forest is small, I ask you. I have stopped only to eat my picnic lunch and to drink water. The sign in the parking lot at the start of today's hike said that Orthez was a two-hour walk away. I have been walking four hours, at least. As I reach the early houses of Orthez, I can see that I have a couple more miles to get to the *centre ville* and the Office de Tourisme. All is well. I changed to my hiking sandals miles back, at the utter insistence of my toes. I carry down *Rue Moncade* past an old keep and castle tower to my right and then down *Rue de l'Horloge* past the *Hotel de la Lune* where I hope to spend the night. I am walking past charming Basque-style houses, whitewashed, and painted in red or green trim. The ribbon-narrow streets are lined with huge hanging baskets of bright yellow flowers like a welcoming committee. *Accueil!* I am making a bee line to the tourist office to sign up for a bed at the *gite* once it opens late afternoon. There are two dormitory rooms, three small beds in each room. By nightfall, I am relieved to report that one of these beds, for the small fee of fifteen euros, belongs to me. My backpack and boots are propped up by my little bed marking my territory. Tonight, all six beds are taken, three French women in one room and me with two men in the other. We are a happy pilgrim community.

In the late Middle Ages, Orthez was the capital of the old *Béarn* region, sitting at the foothills of the Pyrenees, in Basque Country. It has a varied and fascinating history. Perhaps one of its most famous inhabitants was Gaston III (called Phoebus or *Fébus*), the Count of Foix. By the mid-fourteenth century, Fébus maintained his vast power and influence by masterfully avoiding the politics of war with either the English or the French kings and their invading armies. By maintaining his neutrality, he was left alone to rule ten territories in the *Béarn*. *Gaston Fébus*, a writer and poet, was one of the last Occitan troubadours in Europe. He wrote *Le Livre de Chasse*, the Book of the Hunt, a beautifully illustrated, early manuscript on hunting. It is thought that he was born at the thirteenth-century *Chateau de Moncade*, its only remnants being *La Tour Moncade*, the octagonal tower jutting out over the horizon, as I first entered Orthez.

The *Hotel de la Lune*, with its bright red outer door and shutters, was also built in the thirteenth century. It accommodated important visitors to the Court at Orthez. Today, pilgrims on the *Voie de Vézelay* climb steep stone stairs to its turret where a huge wooden door gives way to a spiral stone staircase to the second floor and its *gite*. I am awed and honored to be here and to know its unique history.

Just as I stretch out for a nap, I am rousted out of by bed by a suggestion from my Brazilian counterpart and roommate that I must go see the *Eglise Saint-Pierre*, which is open and close by. I take two right turns out of the gite, and I am there, sitting in the glowing, golden light of the nave. Construction on the Church of Saint Peter, an historical monument, began in the thirteenth century. It resumed in 1391 upon the death of *Fébus* when the town received a part of the Count's treasure found in the Tower of Moncade. It is the tallest building in the *Béarn*, sixty feet high, its vault or arched ceiling communing with the stars. The peace I feel sitting here is beyond words. But its history is anything but peaceful. The Wars of Religion had taken their toll. In 1569, the French Huguenots, commanded by the protestant Count of *Montgommery*, massacred the villagers and seized the church. It wasn't returned to its Roman Catholic heritage until 1865. A small, wooden statue of Saint James rests in an alcove. A large sketch of The Martyrdom of Saint Denis hangs nearby. It starkly depicts the legendary saint carrying his head up a hill. Peace, it seems, is subjective. I find it where I can.

Hôtel de la Lune—in Orthez

Heavy rains are forecast for the next four days. This morning, amid the cold drizzle, I walked past the tourist office and then across town to the train station. I purchased a ticket for Saint-Jean-Pied-de-Port, via Bayonne. I also bought a train ticket going four days later from Saint Jean to Biarritz, and finally to Paris. I have decided that I cannot afford to miss the two nights I have booked at Charles de Gaulle Airport in Paris, much less miss my flight home. I also don't want to walk again in sheets of heavy rain. By the time I get to Saint-Jean, it is late in the day, and the *gare* is closing. The tiny train station is buzzing with urgency. Other pilgrims, waiting in a long line, are trying to arrange tickets by bus or train to leave the town for all points beyond. A rail strike starts tomorrow in France for the next four days. I had purchased my tickets just in time to avoid the ensuing chaos.

I am quite familiar with beautiful Saint-Jean-Pied-de-Port (the foot of the pass). The town, called *Donibane Garazi* in the Basque language, has been designated one of *Les Plus Beaux Villages de France*. My sister and I stayed here years ago before we crossed the Pyrenees to begin the Frances Route. Coming back, it feels like I never left it. I cross town and climb the narrow-cobbled *Rue de la Citadelle* heading to the top of the hill and the central pilgrim receiving center, *Le Refuge Municipal Accueil Pelerin*. I have joined a long line of fellow pilgrims who are hanging out in the rain, hoping to find a bed for tonight. I just want to get my pilgrim passport stamped. The volunteers are friendly and helpful, as always. I did not attempt to book at their large pilgrim *gite* because I want to avoid the crowds due to the risks of covid 19. I have been lucky so far. I retrace my steps trying not to slip on the wet, slick pavement until I locate *Gite Ultreia* which is on the left, almost at the bottom of *la Rue de la Citadelle*. For twenty-three euros per night, including *le petit déjeuner*, I have reserved a bed for two nights in an upstairs bedroom of seven spaces. It was the best I could do. Our young host is bilingual and quite helpful. She speaks some English, French, Spanish, and the local

Basque dialect. After a shower and a brief rest, I am heading for a small market to buy food for dinner, but first I want to stop by the church.

L'Eglise de Notre-Dame-du-Bout-du-Pont (the Church of Our Lady of the End of the Bridge) sits at the base of *la Rue de la Citadelle* on the left just before you cross the river *Nive*. From here, pilgrims continue straight on *la Rue d'Espagne* to leave town on the Camino. The lower Valcarlos Route and the Napoleon Route, the high route over the Pyrenees to Roncesvalles (*Roncevaux* in French), are straight ahead. Hola Spain! But now, my focus is on this grand old pilgrim church where so many have offered prayers as they start their journey. Built out of local sandstone on the remains of a primitive church from the thirteenth century, the gothic Church of Our Lady has a distinctive, sparkling, pink hue, even in the mist of the rain. Red votive candles and long white tapers cast an other-worldly glow under a statue of Mother Mary at the front of the nave on the left. Lovely, long, stained-glass windows in blue, red, and green shine high above the front altar. I sit for a long time in the back in the dark, knowing that, most likely, I will never be here again once I leave Saint-Jean. At the *gite,* I am delighted to meet two *pelerines* from Strasbourg. Soon enough, we are all settled in our beds, a total of six of us in the room tonight.

⚜

Today cries out for rest and reflection. The rain is unrelenting but in a way that brings me solace. I don't have to do anything, go anywhere, or be anything. First thing, I visited the church this morning. At noon, I meet my pilgrim friends at the gite to find a restaurant for lunch. We ended up at *Chez Edouard,* the very restaurant my sister and I had enjoyed a most wonderful local dish, *les calamaris en terrine,* years ago. Add *les frites et une salade verte,* and we are all happy as little clams, I mean squid. My friends had already picked this dish off the menu before I could even find it myself. They had also picked out this restaurant as we walked by *Place Charles de Gaulle,* me unable to figure out

Church of our Lady—Saint-Jean-Pied-de-Port

where this restaurant from years past was located. Synchronicity is so much fun, especially if it is allowed to work its magic free of interference.

Mes amies de Strasbourg are leaving Saint-Jean tomorrow morning to cross the Pyrenees on the low route, rain or shine. And *Gîte Ultreia* will be closed to give our host some much-needed time off. This is still high season on the Camino, and the town is a bustle of activity. Pilgrims and tourists alike are coming and going endlessly. But the breadcrumbs have already been laid out. An Australian couple staying at our current *gîte* booked a room at a *chambre d'hote* just up the street at *28 Rue de la Citadelle.* They keep drumming it in my head, "No. 28, remember number 28." Reaching Marc at No. 28, I, too, reserve a room, along with *le petit déjeuner* and access to the kitchen, for the next two nights. I feel quite fortunate to get it. And since synchronicity is still tapping on my shoulder, I also happen to run into my pilgrim friend, Kristen, at an ATM, for one last hug as we part ways. She is heading home to Holland on a bus, and I leave for Paris in two days, just as the rail strike ends.

Tonight, my friends head out for dinner at a popular restaurant for pilgrims three doors up. I have opted to have instant pasta and fruit and retire early. There is peace in solitude; I savor it more and more. But, as darkness descends, a young friendly American man from Oklahoma takes the last bed in our room. He knows nothing about the Camino and, on a lark, got to Saint-Jean tonight, planning to walk the high route tomorrow morning. Since he has no time restraints as my two friends do, I encourage him to wait a day or two until the weather improves. Walking the high Napoleon Route across the Pyrenees is folly in bad weather due to low visibility in the peaks. The Napoleon Route closes often due to fog or snow, so why leave tomorrow morning? It might be worth the wait to see the wild mares and their fawns frolicking in the mountain vales and the rainbows and not just dense fog two feet in front of you. I smile to myself. The experience of an old, seasoned pilgrim like me brings

Walking West on the Camino—on the Vézelay Route   121

wisdom, but so does the spontaneity and wild freedom of youth. Whatever choice he makes will be the right one for him.

Rain is pelting down on my cape as I climb the glistening cobblestones to reach No. 28. Marc and his wife are impeccable hosts. I have settled into a lovely upper room overlooking the terra cotta rooftops of the town. In a break in the rain, I gaze out a window in time to see a little calico cat unsuccessfully stalking a bird perched high on a roof. I can't help but wonder how this cat got up here. My time is spent at the church, but also taking naps. The raindrops tap their tranquil melody on the skylight above my bed. I am sad to leave Saint-Jean-Pied-de-Port knowing I might never get here again. I also know that my memories of it will soothe me at night as I fall asleep gazing at the stars.

Two days hence, I am headed on a packed train full of pilgrims, first to Biarritz for a brief changeover, and then to Paris Montparnasse. Sweet reality has set in that I have completed my journey on the *Voie de Vézelay*. I am ready to go home. Once in Paris, I cross several blocks to the Central Metro Station to purchase a ticket for the metro north to the Charles de Gaulle Airport. It is Saturday, and, unfortunately, the subway line stops short of the airport today, and we are directed onto buses to take us to the airport. Chaos and confusion finally give way to order. Once at the airport, I figure out the hard way how to get to the Roissy Ibis Hotel by Terminal 3. It took me an hour to find it, after finally jumping into a taxi. All I needed to do was to take the free airport shuttle to the end of the line at Rossypole. *Voila!* The Ibis is a popular hotel, no doubt busy year-round, for all those travelers passing through Paris to all points across the globe. I have a nice, comfortable room for two nights here which I had booked before I left home. And yes, it is still raining. Tonight, the patter of the rain at the window, mixed with the hum of airport traffic, lulls me to sleep.

This is my only day in Paris. I am tempted to stay in my bed since it is supposed to rain all day long. Heavy rain greets me as I awake. But after *le petit déjeuner*, I have adjusted my attitude and have made the rain my friend. I am now a willing prisoner of Paris and of the cold rain. La, la, la! I walk across to a bus terminal and discover, mostly by accident, that a bus leaves for Paris from there almost every hour. I purchase a ticket to get off at the Palace Garnier, the Opera House, in the eighth arrondissement. We wind our way, at a snail's pace, in and out of all the airport terminals picking up other passengers, eventually to reach central Paris. And if I can just remember where I got dropped off exactly, I can ride that bus line back to the airport easily enough.

It seems only fitting to end my pilgrimage on the Vézelay Route in Paris at *L'église de la Sainte-Marie-Madeleine*. The bus driver offers to show me how to catch another bus closer to the church, but I decline. I wish to walk in the rain, so he kindly points me in the direction of the church. La Madeleine is another UNESCO World Heritage Site, and although it is currently undergoing reparations, its fundamental splendor still shines forth. In 1801, after the Napoleonic Wars, Napoleon initially commissioned a type of pantheon here in honor of his armies. By 1842, however, the site was transformed into a church to honor Mary Magdalene. As I approach it, walking up Place de la Madeleine, I am greeted by what looks like a Greek temple surrounded by large glistening, white columns. Statues of male and female saints stand high on the building. It is a breathtaking masterpiece. Built in the Neoclassical style, more columns surround the altar at the front of the nave. I am struck by the beauty of huge, golden chandeliers that shine a dim other-worldly light on a white marble statue of the Magdalen. Called "The Ecstasy of Mary Magdalene" by Carlo Marochetti, Mary Magdalene is ascending into heaven, transported by three great angels. Her arms are outstretched like those of Jesus in his own ascension. Behind her is a curious series of high frescoes painted in gold and pastel hues of the Christ of the Resurrection. He is accompanied by the first disciples and missionaries who lived and preached in Gaul, in the South of France. Among others, there is Mary Magdalene, her sister Saint Martha, Saint Front (the first bishop of Périgueux), and Saint Lazare (Lazarus) who founded the first church in Marseilles.

I am reminded of the hauntingly, beautiful legend of that small boat that washed ashore in the marshes of the Camargue in southern France with some interesting figures onboard. The seaside village of Saintes-Maries-de-la-Mer pays homage to the event. At the medieval Church of *Notre-Dame-de-la-Mer* there, the Blessed Mary is venerated, as well as the relics of the three Marys: Mary Magdalene; Mary Jacobé, called Mary of Clopas, the sister or sister-in-law of Mary; and Mary Salomé. And once a year on May twenty-fifth, the Roma gypsies turn out in mass for a festival celebrating their patron saint, Sara. She, who washed ashore in the boat with the others, is also venerated here. A black madonna stands in the church, perhaps a symbol of the veiled mysteries of the grail legend, so prevalent in the Middle Ages among the troubadours and bards, especially in Provence.

Our world seeks the return of the divine feminine, embodied in the Magdalen. Although I have diverted us from our path once again, the tale of my journey on the Vézelay Route would require nothing less. And so it is.

Fini

Epilogue

My sister, Marcia, and I are planning to return to France in May of 2023 for an Artists and Writers Residency at the beautiful Chateau d'Orquevaux just southeast of Paris. We also hope to visit the South of France, specifically, Aix-en-Provence and Arles. The Arles Route, one of the four great medieval French routes on the Camino, calls us to itself. It's no surprise, is it? From Arles, the Via Tolosana winds its way through the marshes of the Camargue to Montpellier, through the heights of the Languedoc to Toulouse, and then farther southward to Pau, crossing the Pyrenees at the Somport Pass, toward Santiago de Compostela. Perhaps a walk to Montpellier and to the village of Saint-Guilhem-le-Désert, twenty-five miles beyond, will be all we can accomplish on this trip. Saint-Guilhem, a UNESCO World Heritage Site, is nestled high in the rocky crags of the wild Hérault Gorges.

Or we might opt for a day or two on the Arles Route and then travel to the heart of *la région de la Madeleine,* to the seaside village of Saintes-Maries-de-la-Mer and to the Grotto and Basilica in Saint-Maximin-la-Sainte-Baume.

And, most importantly, I trust that I am shedding the ego and drama of life, simply leaving it behind and walking on. I hope that I, too, have transformed as the Magdalen might have done in a cave in the South of France. As legend has it.

www.ingramcontent.com/pod-product-compliance
Lightning Source LLC
Chambersburg PA
CBHW051600010526
44118CB00023B/2771